BEER
AND GOOD FOOD

Bob and Coleen Simmons

BRISTOL PUBLISHING ENTERPRISES
San Leandro, California

a nitty gritty® cookbook

Printed in the United States of America.

ISBN 1-55867-177-3

Cover design: Frank J. Paredes
Cover photography: John A. Benson
Food stylist: Susan Massey

CONTENTS

THE BEER REVOLUTION

We are in the middle of a revolution. A Beer revolution! It started very slowly in the '60s, accelerated slightly in the '70s, gathered steam in the '80s and exploded in the '90s.

Beer, like bread, is made from fermented grains. Both predate written history. We can only speculate whether nomadic tribes started settling in one place to raise grain, or started to raise grain after they settled down. The first beers were probably made from bread moistened and fermented by airborne yeasts. Almost every grain-producing culture in history has produced beer.

At the turn of the century, this country produced a lot of very good beer. Each immigrant community, whether German, Irish, English or Central European, had at least one small brewery that fashioned beer similar to that made in their homeland. These breweries supplied a small geographic area. Some producers eventually bottled a beer or two, which could be purchased locally, and sometimes regionally.

Next came Prohibition, which caused many of the breweries to close. Some survived by producing "near beer," or malt syrup, for the home brewer. When Prohibition was repealed in 1933, many breweries found themselves with outmoded equipment, a deficiency of talented brewers and a public that wasn't consuming nearly as much beer as before. The Depression only made things worse. During the dry years, technology and transportation had made great strides. Mechanical refrigeration had become more widespread. The breweries that did survive were often gobbled up by regional breweries, which found it more economical to run a large operation and ship great distances by refrigerated rail car or truck.

World War II created a demand for large quantities of bottled and canned beer for our armed services. Larger breweries could meet this demand and had efficient bottling facilities. The preferred beer seemed to be light in color, high in carbonation and low in alcohol. It didn't have enough character to offend palates that were not accustomed to the taste of stronger, more flavorful malt beverages. Imported barley and hops were scarce, so corn and rice along with local barley were used to make the beers. After the war, servicemen and tourists returning from Europe longed for the styles of beers they tasted in Europe and a small demand for similar beers began.

Huge advertising budgets were devoted to convincing the public that the lighter style was what beer should be. Many campaigns focused on the brewing water as much as the character of the beer. More and more small and/or regional breweries were acquired by bigger breweries or went out of business. There wasn't a great difference in the major brands. A few of the more robust beers were required to be labeled as "malt liquor" because of the high alcohol content, but didn't capture a very large share of the market. Malt liquor was often purchased as much for its added "kick" as for its flavor. Rarely did ads suggest serving beer with a meal.

In the '60s there was a little more time and money, and people started a pattern of more adventuresome eating and drinking. Julia Child found an eager audience, and dedicated individuals started small wineries with a goal of making more distinctive, higher quality wines than those being produced by the high-volume standard wineries. The beer industry would soon follow suit.

It took another 20 years for microbreweries to take off. Home brewing had been popular and legal during Prohibition, but waned after repeal. A few adventurous souls continued to brew beer as a hobby. Some made very good beer, but obtaining quality ingredients was difficult. In the early '80s, some of the best home brewers opened bars or restaurants and started selling their beer. In the mid-80s, a few started bottling and selling locally to restaurants and retail outlets. This started the microbrewery explosion.

The best of the brews found an appreciative market. High-quality malt and hops became more readily available, as did information on and equipment for brewing beer. The explosion continues. Every week new "brew pubs" open, and established ones start bottling some of their better brews and move into the microbrewery domain. Major breweries test-market new styles, sometimes under an identifiable name, sometimes with nothing to identify the producer. Poorly managed operations go out of business, but there is always new capital and new talent to fill the marketplace with a wonderful array of interesting, well-made new products. Who knows where it will all end? We live in very exciting times and as long as one keeps an open mind and a spirit of adventure, the taste delights are endless!

ABOUT BEER

DEFINING BEER

Beer is usually thought to be a fermented alcoholic beverage made primary from malted barley or other grains and flavored with hops. However, beer can be defined as any alcoholic beverage made by fermenting grains, and as a result, there are several interesting styles of beer being produced today. Beer is usually about 5% alcohol by volume (4% by weight). Its fermentation is produced by mixing yeasts with the grains.

Beer can be divided into two broad styles: ales and lagers. Ales are fermented at a high temperature for a short period of time and the yeast rises to the top of the fermenting liquid. Ales tend to have complex flavors developed during their warm, quick fermentation, which results in fruity, buttery and spicy notes in the finished beer. Some ales are *bottle conditioned*. In this technique, a small amount of sugar is added to the bottle just before capping so that a slow fermentation continues in the bottle,which allows the ale to improve with age. Lagers, on the other hand, are fermented at a lower temperature for a longer period of time, and the yeast tends to settle to the bottom of the fermenting liquid. Lagers have lighter, less complex flavors with malt and hop flavors dominating.

These are not simple cut-and-dry definitions, however. There are myriad exceptions and hybrids. *Brewmasters*, like winemakers, are artists and are constantly experimenting and striving to make something unusual. Whole books are devoted to exploring beer styles and over 60 distinct styles have been defined. Some of the most common styles on the market follow.

North American Lager: Produced by major U.S. and Canadian megabreweries, this type of beer is pale in color and highly carbonated. The flavor has a hint of malt, a faint bitterness and often a slightly sweet finish. Use this simple beer in batters, with snacks, as an accompaniment to highly spiced foods and as a thirst quencher.

Pilsner Lager: Similar to North American Lager, pilsner is made with more malt, more hops and less carbonation. It pairs well with seafood, chicken and veal dishes with light sauces.

Dark Lager: This is made with dark-roasted malt and is fermented at a low temperature using lager yeast. Dark lager has a distinct malty character, but it is lighter and cleaner-tasting than ale. Drink it with pizza, Mexican food or smoked fish.

Marzen: Lagers of this general style are also labeled as *Oktoberfest*, *Dunkel* or *Vienna* beer. These dark beers tend to be maltier and have more character than pilsners. Serve with roast pork, sausages, grilled steak and hearty pizza.

Bock: This lager, traditionally brewed in the springtime, is very malty, dark, sweet and high in alcohol. It is sometimes highly flavored with hops. Lighter bocks go well with aged cheeses, hamburgers and full-flavored stews. *Double bock* and *Triple Bock* have even more malt character and are most often enjoyed by themselves as an after-dinner drink, rather than paired with food.

Wheat Beer: Wheat beer is made by replacing a significant portion of the barley malt with wheat or wheat malt during the brewing process. It is made in Belgium, Germany and the U.S. In Belgium, it is called *wit* (white) beer and in Germany it is called *weiss* (white) or *weisen* (wheat) beer. Serve with grilled chicken, smoked fish and barbecue.

Hefe-weisen: This light-bodied, effervescent lager is brewed with up to half malted wheat. It often has lemon or clove flavors. Most are only lightly flavored with hops and are sometimes quite cloudy. Hefe-weisen is very refreshing as a summer drink and goes particularly well with fish and shellfish.

Pale Ale: In North America, this ale has a medium-gold color, a malty flavor and fruity overtones. It varies widely from producer to producer. Some are lightly hopped, while others heavily hopped and quite bitter. Serve pale ale with barbecued pork or grilled salmon. In England, pale ale is very different. It can range in color from golden brown to copper to very dark brown. "Pale" refers to the fact that it is sparkling clear, never cloudy.

Bitter: The most popular beer style in England, bitter is usually served on draft from the tap. It is very similar to English pale ale, which is usually bottled. Both are fruity, full-flavored ales that are delicious with chicken, pork and vegetarian entrées.

India Pale Ale (IPA): This beer is like pale ale, but usually maltier, higher in alcohol and richer in hop character. It complements beef, lamb, curries and spicy dishes.

Amber Ale: The color of amber ale ranges from medium amber to deep copper. It is maltier than pale ale and is often highly hopped. Its full-bodied, sometimes slightly sweet flavor goes well with roasted poultry, veal dishes and hamburgers.

Brown Ale: Brown ale is a sweet and malty English-style ale. It's delicious with duck and pork dishes, and can be used in salad dressings.

Cream Ale: Also called "lager ale," cream ale is warm-fermented in the English manner, then allowed to mellow at lager temperatures. Cream ale is usually very pale in color, sharing qualities of both pilsner and pale ale. Serve it with light dishes, fish or chicken with light sauces.

Scotch Ale: This is a dark version of amber ale with a higher alcohol content. Its strong malty flavors make it a good choice to serve with game, roast beef, ham, smoked poultry and strong cheeses.

Abbey or **Trappist Ales**: These ales are produced by monastic orders, often with recipes dating back thousands of years. Only six orders still produce beer for the commercial market. These ales are top fermented, bottle conditioned and have fruity, complex flavors. Serve with rich dishes, game, cheese or alone.

Porter: This very old English-style dark brown ale has pronounced malt flavors. Porter goes well with a variety of meat and cheese dishes.

Stout: Darker and heavier than porter, stout is made with highly roasted dark malt, which sometimes lends undertones of coffee or chocolate. Styles range from extremely smoky and bitter, to sweet and almost cognac-like. *Oatmeal Stout* is a light-style stout. Pair stout with oysters, smoked poultry, ham and cheeses.

Lambic: True lambic is naturally fermented in Belgium by wild yeast strains that inhabit the breweries. Most lambics on the market are fruit-flavored and quite intense. Raspberry, cherry and apricot lambics are worth seeking out. Lambic has only a small amount of hops to allow the fruit's characteristics to show through. Lambics are usually drunk by themselves or incorporated into desserts.

Celebration Beers: These are typically made once a year for the holidays and can vary widely from year to year. Generally, these are complex, full-bodied ales, often flavored with spices, herbs or fruit. They're best savored by themselves.

Specialty Beers: In the continuing effort to make something unusual, brewmasters constantly create new types of beers. Smoked beer, hot chile beer, pumpkin beer and spice beer are a few of the more off-beat examples. Some of the fruit-flavored ales, such as *Weizenberry* and *Honey-Raspberry Ale*, both flavored with raspberries, are delicious. Most of these uncommon beers are better served by themselves instead of with a meal. In small quantities, some can be intriguing and delicious. Try to buy single bottles to taste. You can always buy more if you really like them.

BUYING AND STORING BEER

Beer, with very few exceptions, is at its best the day it is bottled. In addition to time, heat and light are the enemies of beer. Brown or green bottles protect beer from light, and refrigerated shipping containers protect beer from heat. Beers that are high in alcohol and with pronounced malt and hops tend to stay fresh longer. Recently, large breweries have begun dating each can or bottle of beer, which helps consumers to be certain that the products are fresh. Old, light-struck or "cooked" beer will at the very best have diminished flavor and interest, and at the worst have a metallic taste and a "skunky" aroma. To increase your chances of enjoying fresh beer, here are some hints.

- Buy from a store that sells a high volume of beer. This is especially important when purchasing imported and micro-brewed beer.
- Buy beer from the refrigerator case instead of off the shelf. This assures that for at least part of its life, the beer has been well stored.
- Buy only the quantity that you will drink in a few weeks and, if possible, refrigerate the beer until it is consumed. Failing this, store the beer in a cool, dark place.
- Join a "beer of the month" program. Each month you will automatically receive several bottles of interesting, fresh beer. Beer magazines, food magazines and the internet are all good places to find a program that suits you.

SERVING BEER

Color, clarity, bubble size and "head" are the first things one notices about a newly poured beer. A sparkling clean glass is important for this visual inspection. Purists never wash beer glasses with detergent, but we find that glasses washed in the dishwasher with a high-quality dishwasher soap are fine for serving beer. If you hand-wash glasses, be certain to rinse them very well to remove any residue from the detergent. A tablespoon of washing soda in the dishwater will cut oily or soapy films. Air-dry the glasses on a rack, or dry them with a very clean dishtowel.

There are many shapes, sizes and styles of beer glasses, some of which are traditional to a region, or even associated with a particular brew. Glasses can vary from short to tall, mug-style to stemware, light to heavy and with hourglass or tulip shapes. All of these styles have their devotees. Our favorite is a generous-sized tulip-shaped wine glass, which shows off the beer's attributes and concentrates the aroma. You can hold the glass by the stem so that the warmth of your hand does not change the temperature of the beer.

Serving temperature is very important. Serious beer drinkers almost never serve icy cold beer with food. In general, lighter American lager and pilsner should be served cool, at about 40° to 45°. Ales should be served a little warmer, about 45° to 50°. Porters and stouts are best when drunk a little warmer, about 50° to 55°. On a very warm day, serve beer a little cooler, and on a wintry night, a little warmer. Remove beer from the refrigerator a few minutes before serving, depending on the temperature of your refrigerator, and let it warm slightly. You may have to let porters and stouts warm for 20 to 25 minutes. Plan on at least 12 ounces per person when serving beer with a meal. Have a few bottles in reserve in case the beer is a great hit.

TASTING BEER

A great way to entertain is to have a beer tasting. The simplest tastings are very little work and a lot of fun. Select 5 or 6 beers with a theme in mind, and take into account the experience and sophistication of your guests. If they haven't tasted many beers other than North American lager, perhaps select three European lagers and three pale ales. This will lead them gently into appreciating more flavorful beer. The more experienced would appreciate tasting 6 well-selected English ales, assorted porters and stouts or a group of related microbrews. Summer is the ideal time to taste an assortment of hefe-weisens and wheat beers.

When approaching any unfamiliar beer, you will want to look at it for color and clarity; check the aroma by smelling it; taste it, noticing body and aftertaste; and then decide on its overall quality. As with wine tasting, there is a special vocabulary to describe beer appearance, aromas and flavors.

Color: Beer color is primarily dependent on the darkness of the malt used in brewing. American lager colors typically range from pale straw to light gold, with European pilsner ranging a bit more toward medium gold. Ales can be light amber, copper or medium-brown in hue. Bocks, porters and stouts are generally medium-brown to almost black in color. A beer's appearance can give an indication of taste, but the darkest beers may not necessarily have the most pronounced flavors.

Bubble size: A well-made beer will have very small bubbles that rise to the surface in a steady stream. Inexpensive beers, those that are carbonated to the desired level before shipping, usually have larger, short-lived bubbles. A creamy and long-lasting *head* (the thick foam that rises to the top of the glass after pouring) is a desirable characteristic.

Clarity: Most commercial beers are sparkling clear. Some wheat beers, such as hefe-weisen, are exceptions, as are a few bottle-conditioned ales. The yeast cells, which make a beer cloudy, are filtered out before bottling both for aesthetic reasons and to prevent a secondary fermentation in the bottle during shipping. An unexpected fermentation could change the beer's flavor and possibly produce enough pressure to explode the bottle.

Aroma: Beer aromas dissipate rapidly, so sniff the beer immediately after pouring while the head is still forming. Depending on how much and how dark the malt that was used, aromas can range from faintly floral to intensely coffee- or chocolate-like. Hop aromas can be described as floral, grassy, spicy or citrusy. The variety of hops, the amount used, and when the hops were added during brewing also impact the aroma. Be wary of "off" aromas, as they may hint at unpleasant flavors.

Flavor: A beer's flavor comes primarily from the malt, hops and fermentation by-products. Malt contributes toasty, nutty, roasted, caramel or coffee-like flavors. Very highly roasted malt can also add a degree of bitterness, as in stouts. Hops provide various degrees of grassy, piney, floral, citrus and herbal flavors. Fermentation by-products can produce fruity, buttery or yeasty or alcoholic sensations, as well as unwanted flavors and "off" tastes.

Body: Body relates to the textural sensation in the mouth. For example, a light-bodied beer would feel more like water in your mouth, while a full-bodied beer would feel more like milk. Body is largely dependent on unfermented sugars and alcoholic strength.

Aftertaste: The aftertaste of beer should be clean, balanced and lingering. Heavier-bodied brews tend to have a more pronounced aftertaste.

Overall quality: This category is somewhat subjective. Ask yourself: Do I like it? Would I buy it? When would I drink it? Would it accompany food? If so, what food?

Beer goes well with most foods. It can emphasize or contrast with flavors in a particular dish the same way wine does. However, beer is often less expensive and more accessible than wine. Mouth-searing curries, hot chiles, piquant barbecue dishes and spicy Chinese food cry for a cooling, light, fizzy lager or pilsner. Lemony wheat beers and creamy porters complement grilled seafood and poultry. The Irish consider stout and trout or oysters to be a classic combination. We have included ideas and recipes for wonderfully delicious foods to go with beer. Many of the recipes have beer as an ingredient, and all have been designed to be a better companion for beer than they are for wine. See pages 161 to 166 for some exciting menu ideas. The continuing search for perfect food and beer matches can be a pleasurable lifelong pursuit.

BEER WITH APPETIZERS

PAIRING BEER WITH APPETIZERS

Cold beer and appetizers make a splendid start to any party or impromptu afternoon festivity. There are beers for every season, time and occasion.

Drink a chilled wheat beer or hefe-weizen, or a dry stout with *Shrimp Boiled in Beer* or *Steamed Manila Clams*. Belgium's Duvel ale is complex, almost champagne-like, and is delicious with shellfish appetizers. A crisp Alsatian bitter or a German lager will nicely complement *Onion Tart*. Both *Blue Cheese Walnut Spread* and *Stuffed Edam Cheese* can serve as an appetizer or cheese course, accompanied by a rich dark porter or stout.

Many of these appetizers can be made ahead of time for ease when entertaining. *Lager-Marinated Mushrooms*, *Spicy Indian Eggplant Spread*, *Blue Cheese Walnut Spread* and *Stuffed Edam Cheese* all keep well in the refrigerator for several days.

Snack foods such as pretzels, popcorn, chips, dips, radishes, olives, pickles and nuts of all kinds go better with with beer than they do with wine. Beer pairs perfectly with deli foods, too, for quick party fare. Serve a wheat beer, pilsner or brown ale with smoked salmon or trout. Scotch ale, amber ale or golden pilsner match well with cold cuts and sausages. There is no limit to pairing great beer with great food. For an easy appetizer party, serve a variety of beers and appetizers and let your guests decide on their own favorite combinations. Everyone will enjoy the challenge.

BEER CHEESE PUFFS

These savory little puffs can be served hot out of the oven or cooled slightly. Drink your favorite pilsner or ale.

1 cup amber ale or lager
1/3 cup butter
pinch cayenne pepper
1/2 tsp. dry mustard
1/2 tsp. curry powder

1/4 tsp. salt
1 cup flour
4 eggs
1/2 cup finely shredded Gruyère or Swiss
   cheese

Heat oven to 425°. Place ale, butter, cayenne, mustard, curry powder and salt in a small saucepan. Bring to a boil over high heat. Reduce heat to low and stir in flour until well absorbed. Remove pan from heat and add eggs one at a time, beating until incorporated. Stir in cheese. Drop tablespoons of mixture 1 to 2 inches apart on parchment- or foil-lined baking sheets. Bake for 10 minutes. Reduce oven heat to 375° and bake for 20 to 25 minutes, until lightly browned and crisp. Turn off oven. Remove puffs from oven and make a small slit in sides of puffs with a sharp knife to release steam. Return puffs to oven for 5 to 10 minutes to dry centers. Serve warm.

BLUE CHEESE WALNUT SPREAD

Serve this piquant cheese spread with celery sticks, apple slices or crackers. Use a food processor to chop the walnuts. This spread can be made a day or two before serving so the flavors have a chance to blend. Drink a mellow stout.

4 oz. cream cheese, room temperature
4 oz. blue-veined cheese, room
    temperature
2-3 tbs. porter or amber ale
3-4 drops Tabasco Sauce
1 cup walnuts, toasted, finely chopped

Belgian brewers are the most fanatic about glassware. Many major breweries insist that taverns serve their beer in a specific, often unique, glass.

Mix together cream cheese and blue cheese until smooth and well mixed. Add 2 tbs. of the porter and Tabasco and mix well. Set aside ¼ cup of the chopped walnuts; mix remaining walnuts with cheese mixture. If mixture is too firm to spread, stir in up to 1 tbs. porter. Spoon cheese spread into a small crock or bowl and sprinkle with remaining walnuts. Cover and refrigerate for 1 to 2 days. For easier spreading, remove mixture from refrigerator about 1 hour before serving.

SPICY INDIAN EGGPLANT SPREAD

Makes about 2 cups

Drink an India pale ale or Jamaican Red Stripe beer with this flavorful spread. Use **Pita Chips**, *page 23, crisp crackers, or pieces of chapati or whole wheat or flour tortillas as dippers. Use only half of a jalapeño if you want a less spicy dish. Garam masala is an Indian spice blend that can be found in Indian markets or specialty food stores.*

1 eggplant, about 1 lb.
1 tsp. vegetable oil
2 tbs. butter
1 small onion, finely chopped
2 cloves garlic, finely chopped
1 inch ginger root, peeled, finely chopped
1 jalapeño chile, seeded, finely chopped
1/2 tsp. turmeric

1/2 tsp. ground cumin
1/2 tsp. chili powder
1/2 tsp. garam masala, optional
2 plum tomatoes, cored, coarsely chopped
1 tbs. lemon juice
1 tsp. toasted sesame oil
salt and freshly ground pepper
1/4 cup chopped fresh cilantro leaves

Heat oven to 400°. Cut eggplant in half lengthwise and lightly rub skin with vegetable oil. Place eggplant halves cut-side down on an oiled baking sheet and bake for 35 to 40 minutes, until very tender when pierced with a knife. When cool enough to handle, pull skin from eggplant and discard. Scoop out as many seeds as possible and discard. Coarsely chop eggplant pulp and set aside.

Melt butter in a skillet over medium heat and sauté onion for about 8 to 10 minutes, until soft and golden brown. Add garlic, ginger, chile and spices and cook for about 1 to 2 minutes, until spices release their fragrance. Add tomato pieces and eggplant. Reduce heat to low and cook for 5 to 6 minutes, until tomato is softened. Stir in lemon juice and sesame oil. Check seasonings and add salt and freshly ground pepper. Sprinkle with cilantro leaves just before serving. Serve slightly warm or at room temperature.

Louis Pasteur's fermentation studies made modern brewing possible. He identified the living organisms that cause fermentation, which eventually led to the development of pure yeast strains. Far more consistent beers were brewed as a result.

MIDDLE EASTERN APPETIZER PLATE

Servings: 6

*This party dish features a warm savory garbanzo bean and feta cheese base topped with chopped tomatoes, cucumbers and herbs. Serve with crisp **Pita Chips**, page 23, and drink a marzen or pilsner.*

1 can (15 oz.) garbanzo beans
2 cloves garlic, finely chopped
1 small jalapeño chile, seeded, finely chopped
¼ cup lemon juice
2 tsp. toasted sesame oil
1 tsp. ground cumin
3-4 drops Tabasco Sauce
salt and freshly ground pepper to taste
½ cup coarsely crumbled feta cheese
½ cup coarsely grated cucumber, well drained on
    paper towels
½ cup chopped, peeled, seeded fresh tomato
8-10 kalamata olives, pitted, coarsely chopped
2 tbs. finely chopped fresh cilantro
2 tbs. finely chopped fresh mint
Pita Chips, page 23

Beer was used for medication in ancient Egypt. Physicians used beer as an ingredient in many of their pre-scriptions. Throughout European history, beer has often been prescribed for pregnant women and nurs-ing mothers, despite con-temporary warnings against such a practice.

Heat oven to 375°. Drain garbanzo beans, reserving 3 tbs. bean liquid. Place beans in a food processor workbowl with garlic, jalapeño, lemon juice, sesame oil and reserved bean liquid and process until smooth. Add cumin, Tabasco, salt and pepper and process for a few more seconds. Spoon mixture in an even layer on an ovenproof 9-inch serving plate. Sprinkle crumbled feta cheese evenly over garbanzo beans. Bake for 8 to 10 minutes, until cheese softens and starts to melt. Remove from oven. Scatter cucumber, tomato and olives over beans. Sprinkle with fresh cilantro and mint and serve with *Pita Chips*.

PITA CHIPS

Makes 16 chips per pita

*These crisp snacks make great dippers for dips and spreads, such as **Spicy Indian Eggplant Spread**, page 20. They're also very easy to make.*

pita breads

Heat oven to 275°. Cut each pita round into 8 triangular pieces and split each piece horizontally into 2 halves. Place on a baking sheet with the interior-side up. Bake for 12 to 15 minutes, until lightly browned and crisp. Store in an airtight container.

LAGER-MARINATED MUSHROOMS

Serve these with toothpicks, toss with salad greens or add to pasta salads. Accompany with an amber ale or dark lager.

1 lb. small button mushrooms
1 bottle (12 oz.) lager
1 tbs. sugar
1/4 tsp. red pepper flakes
3/4 tsp. dried marjoram
1/2 tsp. salt

1 tbs. sherry vinegar
1 tbs. olive oil
1 tsp. spicy brown or Dijon mustard
1/2 tsp. sugar
salt and freshly ground pepper to taste
2 tbs. chopped fresh parsley

Clean mushrooms and cut stems even with mushroom caps. If using larger mushrooms, cut in half. Combine lager, 1 tbs. sugar, red pepper flakes, marjoram and salt in a 2-quart saucepan and bring to a boil over high heat. Boil mixture for 2 to 3 minutes; add mushrooms and return to a boil. Reduce heat to low and simmer mushrooms, partially covered, for 5 minutes. Remove from heat and cool mushrooms in liquid. Drain cooled mushrooms and place on paper towels to dry.

In a small bowl, whisk together vinegar, olive oil, mustard, 1/2 tsp. sugar, salt, pepper and chopped parsley in a small bowl. Add mushrooms and marinate for 1 to 2 hours in the refrigerator before serving. Remove from refrigerator 30 minutes before serving.

STUFFED EDAM CHEESE

The red wax shell around the cheese makes an attractive serving container for this savory spread. Serve it on a large plate surrounded by crackers or small party rye bread slices. Remove the stuffed cheese from the refrigerator an hour before serving so it will be easy to spread. You will have a little extra cheese filling that can be reserved and used to refill the shell during the party. This keeps well in the refrigerator for several days. Drink a dry stout or porter.

1 whole Edam cheese with red wax
    shell, about 2 lb.
4 oz. light cream cheese, room
    temperature
¼ tsp. white pepper

½ tsp. dry mustard
½ tsp. paprika plus more for garnish
¼ cup amber or pale ale
½ tsp. Worcestershire sauce

With a sharp knife, cut a ¾-inch slice from the top of cheese. With a knife and a sharp teaspoon, carefully scoop cheese from shell, leaving about a ⅜-inch layer around the sides. Place removed cheese in a food processor workbowl and process until finely chopped. Add cream cheese and remaining ingredients and process until smooth. Spoon mixture into cheese shell. Cover and refrigerate for 3 to 4 hours before serving to allow flavors to blend. Sprinkle with a small amount of paprika just before serving.

ONION TART

Caramelized onions and Gruyère cheese bake in a puff pastry crust for a delicious party dish. For ease, use the food processor's 2 mm. slicing disk for the onions. Serve with a German lager or Alsatian bitter.

1 tbs. butter
1 tbs. olive oil
8 cups thinly sliced onions, about 1½ lb.
2 tbs. dry vermouth or white wine
1 tsp. dried thyme
salt and freshly ground pepper to taste
½ cup coarsely shredded Gruyère or Swiss cheese
1 sheet frozen puff pastry, about 8 oz., thawed
3 tbs. grated Parmesan cheese
2-3 tbs. coarsely chopped oil-packed sun-dried tomatoes
8-10 kalamata or 20 niçoise olives, pitted, coarsely chopped

Melt butter and olive oil in a large skillet over low heat. Add onions and toss to coat with butter-oil mixture. Add vermouth, thyme, salt and pepper and cook covered for 25 to 30 minutes, until onions are very soft and lightly browned. Stir once or twice during cooking. Remove cover and continue to cook for 3 to 4 minutes, until liquid has evaporated. Remove from heat and cool for 10 to 15 minutes. Add Gruyère cheese to cooled onions.

Heat oven to 400°. Roll out thawed pastry to a 12-inch square about ¼-inch thick. Sprinkle an ungreased baking sheet with a few drops of water and place pastry on sheet. Turn pastry edges up about ½ inch to make a small raised border. Sprinkle pastry with Parmesan cheese. Spread onion-Gruyère mixture evenly over Parmesan-topped pastry. Top with sun-dried tomato and olive pieces. Bake for 25 to 30 minutes, until pastry is puffed and brown. Cool slightly before serving.

In Munich, Germany, Oktoberfest really begins in mid-September and ends two weeks later, on the first Sunday in October. The beer served at Oktoberfest is called Marzen (March) or Vienna beer. Before mechanical refrigeration, large quantities of lager were brewed in March and stored in cold caves throughout the summer, when the weather was too warm to brew beer.

SANTA FE CHICKEN WINGS

*This baked variation of Buffalo chicken wings pairs well with your favorite Mexican beer or lager. Serve with some guacamole and **Blue Cheese Walnut Spread**, page 19, at your next beer party and provide lots of napkins. The unused wing tips can be used to make homemade chicken stock. Store them in the freezer until needed.*

12 chicken wings, or 24 chicken "drumettes"	3 tbs. vegetable oil
	3 cloves garlic, finely chopped
5 tbs. Tabasco Jalapeño Sauce	1/4 tsp. salt

Rinse chicken wings and pat dry. If using whole chicken wings, cut off tips and reserve for another use. Cut remaining wing pieces into 2 portions at the joint and trim off excess skin. Combine Tabasco, oil, garlic and salt in a small bowl. Place wing pieces in a large, locking plastic bag and add Tabasco mixture. Seal bag well and refrigerate for 3 to 4 hours, turning once or twice.

Heat oven to 400° and line a baking sheet with foil. Remove wings from marinade and place on baking sheet. Bake for 30 to 40 minutes, turning wings over halfway through baking time. Wings should be crisp and brown. Brush wings once or twice during baking with leftover Tabasco mixture. Serve warm.

SAUSAGES COOKED IN APRICOT ALE

This makes a quick appetizer. The fruit-flavored ale gives the sausages a delicious fruity flavor. Serve with a glass of the ale used for cooking or any pale or amber ale.

4-5 Italian sausages, mild or hot
1 cup apricot or honey-raspberry ale
1 tsp. brown sugar

Place sausages in a skillet and add ale and brown sugar. Bring to a boil over high heat. Reduce heat to low, cover and simmer for 10 minutes. Turn sausages once or twice and pierce with a fork to release fat. Remove lid, pour out all but 2 to 3 tbs. liquid, and continue to cook sausages over medium-high heat until nicely browned on all sides. Transfer sausages to a cutting board. When cool enough to handle, slice sausages into ½-inch-thick diagonal slices. Serve with toothpicks.

Match the beer's country of origin with the food's. For example, Mexican beers go well with hot and spicy Mexican food; Asian beers complement the complex flavors of Chinese food; Alsatian beers pair well with rich sausages and onion tart.

MUSTARD-MARINATED SHRIMP

This popular party appetizer can be made ahead and refrigerated for several hours or even overnight. A prepared specialty beer mustard adds delicious flavor to this dish. Drink with a hefe-weisen or pale ale.

1 lb. medium shrimp, peeled, deveined
boiling salted water
2 tbs. spicy brown beer or Dijon mustard
1 large shallot, finely chopped
2 tbs. rice vinegar
1/4 cup olive oil
1/2 tsp. red pepper flakes, or Tabasco Sauce
    to taste
1/2 tsp. dried tarragon
2 tbs. finely chopped fresh parsley
salt and freshly ground pepper to taste

Eighty percent of the beer sold in England is considered "pale ale." When pale ale is served on draught, it is called "bitter."

Cook shrimp in a generous amount of boiling salted water for 2 to 3 minutes, until they just turn pink and are firm to the touch. Drain immediately and briefly rinse with cold water. Combine remaining ingredients in a small bowl and mix well. Pour over warm shrimp and toss to coat. Cool for 5 to 10 minutes, cover tightly and refrigerate for at least 1 hour before serving. Serve with toothpicks.

SHRIMP BOILED IN BEER

*Deveining the shrimp is optional, but it takes less than 20 minutes to tackle a pound of shrimp. Deveined shrimp will absorb more of the beer flavor and the shells will pull off more easily. Add ½ tsp. dried thyme or dill to the shrimp boil if you like. Serve warm or lightly chilled with lots of napkins and **Seafood Cocktail Sauce**, page 33, or **Roasted Chile Pesto Sauce**, page 34.*

1 lb. medium shrimp in shell
2 bottles (12 oz. each) pale ale or lager
1 bay leaf

½ tsp. red pepper flakes
1 tsp. kosher or sea salt
2 tbs. lemon juice

Remove shrimp legs. If desired, cut down the backs of shrimp shells with scissors and pull out the interior vein with a toothpick or sharp knife; leave shells in place around shrimp.

Combine ale with bay leaf, red pepper flakes, salt and lemon juice in a medium saucepan. Bring to a boil over high heat, reduce heat to low and simmer for 5 minutes. Increase heat to high, add shrimp and bring liquid back to a boil. As soon as the shrimp turn pink, about 2 minutes, immediately drain shrimp and pour in a single layer on a large plate or baking sheet to cool. Take care not to overcook shrimp.

STEAMED MANILA CLAMS

These are also delicious in pasta dishes or on pizza. Serve with sliced French bread. Since beer has a tendency to boil over when heated, use a deep-sided pot for this dish. Drink a wheat beer or amber ale.

2 lb. manila clams
¾ cup amber or pale ale
2 tbs. minced shallots

4 quarter-sized pieces ginger root
pinch red pepper flakes
melted butter, optional

Scrub each clam well with a vegetable brush and place in a large bowl. Discard any open clams. Cover clams with lightly salted cold water and let stand for 30 minutes. If you find a lot of sand in the bottom of bowl, repeat soaking process. Combine remaining ingredients in a deep-sided saucepan with a tight-fitting lid, large enough to hold clams. Bring to a rapid boil over high heat and cook for 1 minute; add clams and cover pan. Steam clams over high heat, shaking pan several times. After 3 to 4 minutes, remove lid and check to see if most clams have opened. Use tongs to transfer opened clams to a bowl. Cover pan and continue to cook for 2 more minutes. Remove remaining opened clams, discarding any that are still unopened. Carefully pour off remaining clear cooking liquid into a measuring cup and distribute among small individual bowls. Serve with small bowls of broth and melted butter or *Garlic Butter*, page 33.

SEAFOOD COCKTAIL SAUCE

This is an old-fashioned tomato-flavored dipping sauce. Use it to accompany **Shrimp Boiled in Beer**, *page 31, or other shellfish.*

1 cup ketchup
2 tsp. prepared horseradish sauce
2 tbs. lemon juice
1/2 tsp. Worcestershire sauce
1/8 tsp. celery salt

Combine ingredients in a small bowl. Let stand for 30 minutes to allow flavors to blend.

GARLIC BUTTER

This simple, flavorful sauce is delicious with **Steamed Manila Clams**, *page 32. Sop up any excess with crusty French bread.*

2 cloves garlic, finely chopped   1/2 cup butter

Place chopped garlic and butter in a microwavable bowl. Cook on HIGH until butter melts. Or, place ingredients in a small saucepan and cook over medium-low heat until butter melts. Do not allow garlic to brown.

ROASTED CHILE PESTO SAUCE

*This piquant, smoky sauce is wonderful with **Shrimp Boiled in Beer**, page 31, or grilled fish. Spread a small amount on your hamburgers as they come off the grill. It also makes a zesty pasta sauce or pizza topping.*

2 fresh medium poblano chiles
2 garlic cloves, coarsely chopped
1 tbs. lime juice
¼ cup vegetable oil
¼ cup coarsely chopped cilantro leaves
2 tbs. toasted pine nuts

½ tsp. chopped chipotle chile in adobo
  sauce, or dash red pepper flakes
½ tsp. salt
freshly ground pepper to taste
1-2 tbs. water, optional

Heat broiler. Place chiles on a rack on a foil-lined baking sheet. Broil about 6 inches from heat source until skin is nicely charred; turn occasionally to char all sides. Place in a large covered bowl and steam for 10 to 15 minutes. Pull off charred skin and remove stems and seeds. Coarsely chop peeled chiles and place in a blender container or food processor workbowl with remaining ingredients, except for water. Pulse 5 to 6 times. Process for about 1 minute, until mixture is finely chopped but still has some texture. If sauce seems a little thick, add 1 to 2 tbs. water until sauce reaches dipping consistency. Refrigerate if not serving immediately. Remove from refrigerator 30 minutes before serving.

BEER WITH SOUPS AND SALADS

PAIRING SOUPS AND SALADS WITH BEER

Beer adds complex flavors to hearty vegetable and meat soups. Since long cooking times tend to concentrate beer's bitter or earthy characteristics, choose lighter wheat beers, ales or American lagers when making soups. Taste the beer you plan to use. If there is a pronounced strong hop-flavored or bitter aftertaste, drink the beer with the dish rather than cook with it.

For cool-weather fare, try *Hearty Lentil Soup* with or without sausage, or *Beer and Onion Soup*. *Carrot and Leek Wheat Ale Soup*, which can be served hot or cold, makes a delicious first course for a dinner party, or a summer supper. Portuguese *Caldo Verde* is brimming with potatoes, beans and carrots as well as spicy sausage.

All these soups benefit from an overnight stay in the refrigerator so that the flavors have a chance to blend. They also freeze well, so make them when you have time and put them away for good eating on a cool, rainy day.

A wide variety of salad recipes are included here. *Green Bean and Mushroom Salad*, *German-Style Potato Salad* and *Red Cabbage and Fennel Slaw* make good picnic or barbecue fare. *Spinach Salad with Black Beans and Feta Cheese* functions well as an appetizer at an informal get-together. *Lentil Salad* can serve as a hearty side dish.

CARROT AND LEEK WHEAT ALE SOUP

This creamy, orange-colored soup makes a delicious first course or lunch. Use the food processor's 1 mm. slicing blade to cut the carrots easily. The soup freezes well and can be served hot or cold. If you wish, garnish with some finely grated raw carrot and a mint leaf.

2 medium leeks, about 1 lb., white part
    only
2 tbs. butter
pinch red pepper flakes
1 quarter-sized piece ginger root,
    peeled

grated peel (zest) and juice of 2 oranges
1 lb. carrots, thinly sliced
1 can (14½ oz.) chicken broth
1 bottle (12 oz.) wheat ale
salt and freshly ground pepper to taste
1 tbs. honey

Cut leeks in half lengthwise, rinse well to remove sand and pat dry; slice into ¼-inch half-moons. Melt butter in a large heavy saucepan. Sauté leeks, red pepper flakes and ginger over low heat for 8 to 10 minutes, until leeks are softened. Add orange juice, carrots, chicken broth, ale, salt and pepper. Bring to a boil over high heat, cover, reduce heat to low and simmer for 30 to 40 minutes, until carrots are very tender. Add orange peel and honey and cook for 1 minute. Cool for 10 to 15 minutes. Puree with a blender or food processor until very smooth. Check for seasonings, adding more salt and pepper if needed. Serve in heated soup bowls or refrigerate for 3 to 4 hours and serve cold.

BEER AND ONION SOUP

Servings: 6

A Holland amber ale is great for cooking and drinking. If you prefer, sprinkle cheeses on toasts and place them under the broiler until cheese is melted. Serve on the side with the soup.

2 tbs. vegetable oil
2 tbs. butter
3 lb. yellow onions, thinly sliced
1 tsp. salt plus more to taste
2 tbs. flour
3 cans (14½ oz. each) beef or chicken broth

1 bottle (12 oz.) Holland amber ale or light-style lager
freshly ground pepper to taste
6 large slices bread, ¾-inch thick
1-2 tbs. full-flavored olive oil
⅔ cup shredded Gruyère or Swiss cheese
¼ cup grated Parmesan cheese

Heat oil and butter in a large heavy stockpot. Add onions and salt and cook over medium-low heat, stirring occasionally, for 35 to 40 minutes, until onions are golden brown. Sprinkle flour over onions and cook, stirring, for 2 to 3 minutes. Gradually stir in broth, mixing well; add beer. Bring to a boil over high heat. Reduce heat to low, partially cover and simmer for 30 minutes. Taste and season with salt and pepper.

Heat oven to 350°. Lightly brush bread slices with olive oil, place on a baking sheet and toast in oven until golden brown, turning once. Place 1 slice of toast in each of 6 soup bowls, ladle soup over toast and pass cheeses.

SPLIT PEA SOUP

This old-fashioned soup goes well with an Imperial stout or porter. Puree all or part of the soup with a food processor for a smoother texture. Ham hocks vary in saltiness, so don't add salt until you taste the soup at the end.

2 tbs. butter
1 large onion, finely chopped
2 cloves garlic, finely chopped
1 stalk celery, finely chopped
1 large carrot, finely chopped
dash red pepper flakes, optional
1 lb. split peas, rinsed, sorted
1 bay leaf
2 large sprigs fresh parsley

1 lb. ham hocks or ham bone with
    some meat attached
2 bottles (12 oz. each) Holland amber
    ale or hefe-weisen
5 cups water
freshly ground pepper to taste
salt to taste
1 tsp. finely chopped fresh mint for
    garnish

Heat butter in a large heavy stockpot. Add onion and sauté over medium heat for 3 to 4 minutes. Stir in garlic, celery, carrot and pepper flakes, if using. Cook for 2 to 3 minutes, stirring constantly. Add remaining ingredients, except for salt and mint, and bring to a boil. Reduce heat to low and simmer for 1 to 1¼ hours, until peas are very soft. Remove ham hocks from soup, cool slightly and remove meat from bones. Chop ham finely and return to soup; discard bones. Taste and add salt if needed. Discard parsley stems and bay leaf. Serve soup in warm bowls garnished with mint.

PORTUGUESE "GREEN SOUP" (CALDO VERDE)

This hearty soup features spicy sausage and watercress or spinach. Make it a day ahead for better flavor. Serve with some garlic bread and an amber or pale ale.

2 tbs. olive oil
1 small onion, finely chopped
3 cloves garlic, finely chopped
1 jalapeño chile, seeded, finely chopped
2 medium boiling potatoes, peeled, diced
   (1/2-inch cubes)
1 bottle (12 oz.) amber ale
4 cups chicken broth
1/2 tsp. salt
freshly ground pepper to taste
3-4 chorizo or kielbasa sausages, about 3/4 lb.
1/2 cup water
1 bunch watercress with stems, or 1/2 lb. spinach leaves
1 can (15 oz.) small white beans, drained
2 large carrots, coarsely grated

Beer consumed in moderate quantities is not necessarily fattening. A 12-ounce bottle of beer has about 150 calories, a few calories less than an equal amount of milk, orange juice or wine.

Heat oil in a large heavy saucepan over medium heat. Add onion and sauté for 3 to 4 minutes. Add garlic and jalapeño and cook for 1 to 2 minutes. Add diced potatoes, ale, chicken broth, salt and pepper. Bring to a boil over high heat. Reduce heat to low and simmer for 15 to 20 minutes, until potatoes are soft, but not mushy. Remove soup from heat and cool slightly. Scoop out 1/2 cup potato and vegetable pieces from soup and reserve. Carefully puree remaining soup with a blender or food processor and return to saucepan.

Place sausages in a small skillet. Add water, bring to a boil over high heat and cook for about 5 minutes, until they release some of their fat and the water has evaporated. Finely chop watercress stems and coarsely chop leaves. If using spinach, roll up leaves and cut into thin shreds. Slice sausages into thin rounds. Bring soup back to a boil, stir in watercress, beans, carrots and reserved potato and vegetable pieces and cook for 3 to 4 minutes, just until watercress is wilted and soup is heated through. Divide sausage slices among 6 soup bowls and ladle soup over sausages.

NOTE: If making soup ahead, refrigerate mixture after pureeing. Just before serving, reheat pureed mixture, cook sausages and continue with recipe.

HEARTY LENTIL SOUP WITH SAUSAGE

*This is comfort food — it's perfect for cool-weather meals. The sausages are heated separately and added to the soup as a last-minute accent. This firms the sausages and allows the rendered fat to be discarded. This soup is even better when made a day or two ahead so the flavors have a chance to blend. Serve with a porter or dark lager and **Pepper Jack Cornbread**, page 57.*

1/4 cup olive oil
1 large onion, finely chopped
2 stalks celery, diced
2 medium carrots, diced
6 cloves garlic, finely chopped
1 tsp. ground cumin
1 tsp. Tabasco Sauce, plus more to taste
1 tsp. dried thyme
1 tsp. dry mustard
1/4 cup chopped fresh parsley

1 bay leaf
1 lb. brown lentils, rinsed, sorted
1 bottle (12 oz.) amber or pale ale
1 can (49 1/2 oz.) chicken broth
1 can (14 1/2 oz.) ready-cut tomatoes
1 tsp. salt
freshly ground pepper to taste
1 lb. Polish or garlic sausages
1 cup plain yogurt for garnish
chopped fresh parsley for garnish

Heat olive oil in a 6-quart stockpot over medium heat. Add onion, celery and carrots and sauté for 6 to 8 minutes, until vegetables soften. Add garlic and cumin and cook for 1 minute. Stir in Tabasco, thyme, dry mustard, parsley and bay leaf. Add lentils, beer, chicken broth, tomatoes, salt and pepper. Bring to a boil over high heat. Reduce heat to low, cover and simmer gently for about 35 to 45 minutes, until lentils are tender. Check seasonings, adding more salt, pepper and Tabasco to taste.

Cook sausages on the grill or poach for 5 minutes in simmering water, until heated through. Slice sausages into thin rounds and add to hot soup or place in the bottom of heated soup bowls. Top individual servings of soup with a dollop of yogurt and a sprinkle of parsley, or pass yogurt in a separate dish. Serve immediately.

In Colonial times, beer was a very popular beverage. Native hops were plentiful and other indigenous ingredients, such as maple syrup and spruce needles, were commonly added for flavor, or used to preserve beers. John Adams, Thomas Jefferson and George Washington were all brewers. Martha Jefferson brewed her first beer at Monticello in 1813. George Washington's beer recipe still survives.

AVOCADO CITRUS SALAD

Servings: 4-6

*This bright winter salad makes a great accent for **Jamaican-Style Curried Lamb**, page 128, or any grilled meat. Make this just a few minutes before serving so the avocado doesn't darken. Choose a beer that goes well with the main dish.*

2 large pink grapefruits
2 large oranges
2 ripe avocados
salt and freshly ground pepper to taste
1 small red onion, very thinly sliced, separated into rings
2 tbs. chopped fresh cilantro

Drink highly carbonated beer with spicy food, to cleanse the palate.

With a sharp knife, cut down sides of fruit to remove peel and white pith. Over a serving bowl, cut down both sides of fruit membranes to release fruit segments. Squeeze any juice remaining in membranes into bowl. Cut each fruit segment into bite-sized pieces and place in serving bowl. Cut avocados into 1/2-inch cubes and place in serving bowl. Squeeze any juice remaining on the citrus membranes into bowl. Season with salt and pepper and top with red onion slices and cilantro. Toss well and serve immediately.

GERMAN-STYLE POTATO SALAD

Use thick-sliced smoky bacon in this salad and serve it slightly warm or at room temperature. It is a delicious accompaniment for sausages, grilled meats or cold cuts from the deli. Cook and peel the potatoes and pour the dressing over them while they are still quite warm.

3 thick slices bacon, cut into
   1/2-inch pieces
1 small onion, finely chopped
2 lb. boiling potatoes, boiled until
   tender

1/4 cup cider vinegar
3/4 cup beef broth
salt and freshly ground pepper to taste
2-3 tbs. finely chopped fresh parsley
1-2 tbs. finely chopped fresh chives

Cook bacon in a medium skillet over medium-low heat until browned and crisp; remove from skillet and set aside. Add onion to skillet and cook for 5 to 6 minutes, until onion is soft and translucent. Peel cooked potatoes, cut into quarters and slice thinly. Layer potatoes and bacon in a wide serving bowl, seasoning each layer with salt and pepper. Add vinegar and beef broth to skillet and heat over low heat until just heated through; do not boil. Pour mixture over potatoes and mix gently. Let stand for 15 to 20 minutes, until potatoes absorb liquid. Occasionally tip bowl and spoon liquid over potatoes. Just before serving, sprinkle with parsley and chives.

GREEN BEAN AND MUSHROOM SALAD

Servings: 8

This is an easy and delicious year-round vegetable salad. Use high-quality canned green beans if fresh are not available. If using shiitake mushrooms, be sure to remove the stems. Serve with grilled meats or **Spicy Braised Chicken Legs**, *page 94.*

1½ lb. green beans, stemmed, cut into 1½-inch pieces
boiling salted water
2 tbs. olive oil
½ lb. fresh white, cremini and/or shiitake mushrooms, sliced
¼ cup thinly sliced green onions, white part only
¼ cup cider vinegar
½ cup diced roasted red bell pepper or pimiento
salt and freshly ground pepper to taste

Cook beans in a large pot of boiling salted water for about 10 minutes, until just tender. Drain well and plunge into a bowl of cold water to stop cooking. Drain, pat dry on paper towels and place in a serving bowl. Heat oil over high heat in a medium skillet and sauté sliced mushrooms for 3 to 4 minutes, until they release their liquid. Add green onions and cook for 1 minute. Add vinegar, heat for another minute and pour over beans in serving bowl. Toss together. Add red pepper pieces, salt and pepper and mix well. Serve at room temperature.

RED CABBAGE AND FENNEL SLAW

This colorful salad makes a great accompaniment for barbecued or roasted meats and poultry. Make it a few hours or a day ahead so the flavors have time to blend. Use the food processor's 1 mm. slicing blade for the cabbage and fennel; use the coarse grating blade for the carrots and apple.

½ cup mayonnaise
¼ cup sour cream
¼ cup lemon juice
2 tbs. Dijon mustard
2 tbs. sugar
8 cups thinly sliced red cabbage, about 1½ lb.

1 large fennel bulb, trimmed, thinly sliced
3 large carrots, coarsely grated
1 large green apple, peeled, cored, coarsely grated
salt to taste
generous amount freshly ground pepper

Whisk together mayonnaise, sour cream, lemon juice, mustard and sugar in a small bowl. Place prepared vegetables and apple in a large bowl and immediately toss with mayonnaise mixture until thoroughly coated. Season with salt and pepper. Cover and refrigerate for 3 to 4 hours or overnight. Toss again just before serving.

CAESAR SALAD

A Caesar salad makes a great starter or accompaniment for grilled meats. If you are serving other finger foods at an informal party, make an easy pick-up salad: choose small romaine leaves, leave them whole and toss lightly with the dressing. Be sure to use a good Reggiano Parmesan cheese. When served by itself, this goes well with a hefe-weisen or pale ale.

8-10 oz. romaine lettuce leaves
4 slices French or Italian bread
5 tbs. full-flavored olive oil
2 cloves garlic, sliced
1 tbs. lemon juice

1 tsp. Dijon mustard
1 tbs. anchovy paste, or 3-4 canned
anchovies, drained, finely chopped
salt and freshly ground pepper to taste
1/4 cup freshly grated Parmesan cheese

Wash and thoroughly dry romaine leaves. Wrap with a clean towel and refrigerate. Remove crusts from bread and cut into 1-inch cubes. Heat 2 tbs. of the olive oil with garlic over medium heat in a large skillet. Remove garlic as it browns and discard. When oil is hot, add bread cubes and toss to coat with garlic oil. Cook for 3 to 4 minutes, stirring occasionally, until bread cubes are lightly browned and crisp. Cool on paper towels. Combine remaining 3 tbs. olive oil, lemon juice, mustard, anchovy, salt and pepper in a small bowl and whisk until well blended. Toss lettuce leaves with dressing and sprinkle with Parmesan cheese and croutons. Serve immediately.

SPINACH SALAD WITH BLACK BEANS AND FETA CHEESE

Here is a zesty salad for lunch, a buffet or a barbecue spread. The dressing can be made ahead of time, but dress and toss the salad just before serving. Use baby spinach or curly New Zealand spinach if available. Feta cheese often comes packed in brine; if so, drain it before using.

1 lb. fresh spinach, stems removed, or
    8 oz. spinach leaves
1 tbs. sherry vinegar
3 tbs. full-flavored olive oil
1 small clove garlic, finely chopped
1/4 tsp. ground cumin
salt and freshly ground pepper to taste

1 can (15 oz.) black beans, rinsed,
    drained
1/4 cup diced roasted red bell peppers
1/3 cup crumbled feta cheese
1/4 cup toasted pine nuts or slivered
    almonds
2 tbs. finely chopped fresh mint leaves

Wash spinach leaves well in 2 to 3 changes of water and spin or pat dry. Refrigerate until ready to use. Combine sherry vinegar, olive oil, garlic, cumin, salt and pepper in a food processor workbowl or blender container. Process until well mixed. To assemble, place spinach leaves in a large salad bowl with black beans and red peppers. Toss with salad dressing. Add feta cheese and pine nuts and toss. Sprinkle with fresh mint leaves and serve in individual salad bowls.

GREEN SALAD WITH
MAPLE PORTER-GLAZED SAUSAGE

Servings: 4

Maple porter adds a slight bit of sweetness to the sausages during cooking and is added to a mustard and shallot dressing. The hot sausages are sliced and scattered over greens to make a hearty salad. If maple porter isn't available, substitute a mild or brown ale and add 1 tbs. brown sugar.

3-4 Italian sausages, mild or hot, about ¾ lb.
1¼ cups maple porter
1 tbs. minced shallot
2 tbs. lemon juice
1 tsp. Dijon mustard
3 tbs. maple porter
⅓ cup olive oil
½ tsp. brown sugar
salt and freshly ground pepper to taste
6 cups mixed salad greens
½ cup coarsely shredded Gruyère or Swiss cheese

Coors Brewery in Golden, Colorado is the largest single brewery in the world with a capacity producing over 60 million gallons of beer per year.

Place sausages and porter in a small skillet. Bring to a boil over high heat, reduce heat to medium-high, cover and simmer for 10 minutes. Remove lid, pour off liquid and brown sausages on all sides. Drain on paper towels.

In a blender container or food processor workbowl, combine shallot, lemon juice, mustard, 3 tbs. maple porter, olive oil, brown sugar, salt and pepper and process until well blended. Toss greens with enough dressing to coat leaves. Slice sausages into thin rounds. Place dressed greens on salad plates and top with warm sausage slices and shredded cheese. Serve immediately.

Rice grains that are broken during milling and polishing are called "brewers' rice." Rice is less expensive than malted barley and adds alcoholic strength to beer without adding appreciable flavor or character. Large breweries use some rice in their beers, especially in the "lawnmower" types.

LENTIL SALAD

Unlike other legumes, lentils don't have to be presoaked, and cook fairly quickly. Tiny French green lentils are good for salads because they remain a little firmer than the common brown lentil when cooked. This hearty salad makes a good buffet dish or accompaniment to roasted or grilled meats.

1 cup French green lentils
3 cups water
2 whole cloves
1 small onion, cut in half
1 stalk celery, cut into 3-4 pieces
salt to taste
3 tbs. full-flavored olive oil
⅓ cup finely chopped onion
1 large carrot, finely diced

1 large clove garlic, finely chopped
½ tsp. curry powder
½ tsp. ground cumin
dash red pepper flakes
2-3 tbs. sherry vinegar
1 tsp. brown or Dijon mustard
salt and freshly ground pepper to taste
¼ cup finely chopped fresh parsley

Place lentils in a medium saucepan and cover with water. Stick cloves in onion halves and add to pan with celery. Bring to a boil over high heat. Reduce heat to low, cover and simmer for 20 to 25 minutes. Check lentils frequently for doneness after 15 minutes of cooking. When cooked through, add salt. Remove from heat and set aside.

Add 1 tbs. of the olive oil to a medium skillet. Sauté chopped onion and carrot over medium-high heat for 5 minutes. Add garlic, curry powder, cumin and red pepper flakes and cook for 1 to 2 minutes until their fragrance is released.

Drain lentils, discard onion with cloves and celery and pour into a salad bowl. Stir in warm onion-carrot mixture. In a small bowl whisk together remaining 2 tbs. olive oil, vinegar, mustard, salt and pepper until well blended. Pour over lentil mixture and mix well. Check seasoning. Sprinkle with parsley and serve warm or at room temperature.

When attending or hosting a beer-tasting party, start with light-style beers and progress to heavier styles. Keep an open mind. Sometimes it takes two or three exposures to a new beer type before you begin to appreciate it.

COLD ITALIAN MEAT SALAD

This hearty meat and cheese salad makes a great buffet or party dish. For easy assembly, ask the deli to slice your favorite sandwich meats and cheese 1/8-inch thick. Drink a marzen, amber ale or Alsatian bitter.

2 tbs. spicy brown mustard
2 tbs. sour cream
2 tbs. mayonnaise
1 tbs. lemon juice
freshly ground pepper to taste
1 large tart apple, peeled, cored,
    coarsely grated
3 oz. ham, thinly sliced

3 oz. bologna, thinly sliced
1 oz. salami, thinly sliced
2 oz. Swiss cheese, thinly sliced
2 medium stalks celery, tender
    white parts only
2 medium-sized dill pickles
1 tsp. dried basil
2-3 tbs. finely chopped fresh parsley

In a medium bowl, mix together mustard, sour cream, mayonnaise, lemon juice and pepper. Add grated apple and mix well. Cut meats, cheese, celery and pickles into 1½-inch matchstick-sized pieces and add to bowl. Add basil. Gently toss to combine. Refrigerate until ready to serve. Sprinkle with parsley just before serving.

BEER WITH BREADS AND SIDE DISHES

PAIRING BREADS AND SIDE DISHES WITH BEER

Beer-flavored breads are delicious and easy to make. The yeast in both the beer and the bread contributes to a wonderful aroma during baking. *Cheese-Studded Stout Bread* as well as *Honey Whole Wheat Ale Bread* make great sandwiches and toast. Serve spicy *Pepper Jack Cornbread* or *Caramelized Onion Focaccia* for brunch, supper or anytime you crave bread warm from the oven.

Full-flavored side dishes stand up to grilled entrées and hearty meat preparations. Serve *Mushroom Beer Risotto* or *Stuffed Portobello Mushrooms* for an informal appetizer course. *Potato Gratin* and *Easy Baked Beans* are sturdy side dishes that can round out a meal.

 *Budweiser was named for a town in the Czech Republic called Budejovice, or Budweis in English. There is still a small brewery there that produces a Budweiser brand. For this reason, American Budweiser must be simply labeled "Bud" when sold in Europe.*

PEPPER JACK CORNBREAD

This rich, spicy cornbread is easy to put together and is a delicious accompaniment to barbecue, grilled meat or egg dishes.

1 cup yellow cornmeal
1 cup all-purpose flour
2 tbs. sugar
2 tsp. baking powder
½ tsp. baking soda
½ tsp. ground cumin

1 tsp. salt
1 cup shredded pepper Jack cheese
1 cup buttermilk
3 eggs
3 tbs. unsalted butter, melted

Heat oven to 425°. Generously butter an 8-inch square baking pan. Place cornmeal, flour, sugar, baking powder, soda, cumin and salt in a bowl and stir well to combine. Add shredded cheese and mix well. In another bowl, whisk together buttermilk and eggs; stir in melted butter. Pour buttermilk mixture over dry ingredients and stir until just combined. Pour batter into prepared baking pan. Bake for 25 to 30 minutes, until nicely puffed and lightly browned. Place pan on a cooling rack and cool for a few minutes before cutting and serving.

CHEESE-STUDDED STOUT BREAD

Makes 2 loaves

The small cubes of smoked Gouda cheese melt slightly, but still keep their shape, leaving little pockets of cheese after baking. Use this bread for sandwiches, or toast it for breakfast or lunch.

½ cup oatmeal stout or other dark beer
½ cup milk
1 pkg. active dry yeast
1 tbs. sugar
¼ cup olive oil
3 large eggs
1½ tsp. salt
1 tbs. chili powder
4½-5 cups bread flour
1½ cups cubed smoked Gouda or
    Gruyère cheese, ¼-inch cubes

Matthew Vassar used part of the fortune he had amassed running his Vassar Brewery in Poughkeepsie, NY, to found Vassar College in 1861.

Heat stout and milk in a small saucepan to about 105°. Place yeast, sugar, beer and milk in a mixer bowl and stir to combine. Let stand for about 5 minutes. Add olive oil and eggs and mix well. Add salt, chili powder and flour. With an electric mixer and a dough hook, mix for 5 minutes. Or, stir in flour, turn mixture out onto a board and knead by hand for about 7 to 10 minutes, until dough is smooth and elastic. Transfer dough to a lightly oiled bowl and let rise in a warm, draft-free place until doubled in size, about 1 to 1½ hours.

Gently punch down dough, divide dough in half and flatten each half into a rectangle about 8 x 15 inches. Sprinkle with diced cheese. Roll each piece jelly roll-style into a 9-inch-long cylinder and place in well-oiled 9-x-5-inch loaf pans. Cover and let rise until almost doubled in size.

Heat oven to 375°. Bake bread for 35 to 45 minutes, until nicely browned and bread sounds hollow when tapped. When bread is done, internal temperature will register 210° on an instant-read thermometer. Cool bread in pans for 5 minutes. Turn out onto a rack to cool completely.

CARAMELIZED ONION FOCACCIA

Servings: 6

This delicious, Italian-style bread goes together quickly with a food processor. Serve it warm out of the oven with pasta or a salad, or slice it and use it for a hamburger bun. It makes good sandwiches, too. The caramelized onions go well on their own with grilled meats. Using fast-acting, or instant, yeast eliminates the need to proof the yeast before adding it to the recipe.

CARAMELIZED ONIONS
2 medium-sized red onions
1 tbs. full-flavored olive oil
1/4 cup amber or pale ale
1 tbs. brown sugar

DOUGH
1 cup amber or pale ale, room temperature
1/3 cup light olive oil
1 pkg. fast-acting yeast
1 1/2 tsp. salt
3-3 1/2 cups all-purpose flour
1 tbs. full-flavored olive oil
scant tsp. kosher or coarse sea salt

In the 1870s, beer was marketed through "tied houses." These were comfortable local beer halls that were "tied" to a specific brewery and its product. Tied houses still exist in England, but were outlawed in the United States by the Volstead Act (Prohibition).

Peel onions and cut in half vertically from stem to root. Cut each half into crescent-shaped wedges, about 3/8-inch wide at the broadest part. Separate wedges into individual pieces. Heat olive oil in a medium skillet over low heat. Cook onion in oil for about 25 minutes, stirring occasionally, until very soft. Do not allow to brown. Add beer and brown sugar, increase heat to medium and cook, stirring, until liquid has evaporated. Remove from heat and cool.

For dough, place ale, 1/3 cup olive oil and yeast in a food processor workbowl. Pulse a few times to combine. Add salt and 2 cups of the flour and process for 1 minute. Add 1 cup of the flour and process for another minute. Dough should come together in a nice ball and clean the sides of workbowl, but will be quite soft. If dough doesn't come together, add a small amount of flour. Take care not to overprocess dough, or the heat may kill yeast. Remove dough from workbowl; it will be slightly warm to the touch. Place dough in a lightly oiled bowl and let rise in a warm, draft-free place until doubled in size, about 1 to 1 1/2 hours. Punch down dough, place on a lightly oiled baking sheet and stretch into an oval shape about 1/2-inch thick. Cover with lightly oiled waxed paper and let rise until doubled in size, about 45 minutes.

Heat oven to 400°. Dimple dough surface with your knuckles. Toss onions with 1 tbs. olive oil and distribute evenly over surface of dough. Sprinkle with kosher salt. Bake for about 30 minutes, until nicely puffed and brown. Cool in pan before slicing and serving.

HONEY WHOLE WHEAT ALE BREAD

Makes 1 loaf

This yeasty bread goes together quickly with a food processor. It makes delicious sandwiches or breakfast toast.

1 bottle (12 oz.) pale ale
2 tbs. butter
3 tbs. honey
2 tsp. kosher salt

1 pkg. active dry yeast
1 cup stone-ground whole wheat flour
2¾ cups bread flour
melted butter, optional

Pour beer into a small saucepan. Add butter, honey and salt and bring to a boil, stirring well to combine. Remove from heat and cool to about 100° to 110°. Stir in yeast until dissolved. Place flours in a food processor workbowl and pulse 2 to 3 times to combine. Add ale mixture and process for 2 to 3 minutes until well combined. Spoon dough into a well-buttered 9-x-5-x-4-inch loaf pan, cover with plastic wrap and let rise in a warm place until doubled in size, about 1 hour.

Heat oven to 350°. Brush the top of bread with a small amount of melted butter if desired. Bake for about 1 to 1¼ hours, until a wooden skewer inserted into the middle of bread comes out clean, or until internal temperature registers 210° on an instant-read thermometer. Turn bread out of pan onto a cooling rack until cooled completely.

EASY BAKED BEANS

These are a terrific accompaniment for grilled meats. Double the recipe if cooking for a crowd.

3 thick slices smoky bacon, cut into ½-inch pieces
1 medium onion, chopped
2 tbs. molasses
2 tbs. brown sugar, packed
1 tbs. Dijon or spicy brown mustard
2 tbs. tomato paste
1 tsp. Worcestershire sauce
2 cans (15 oz. each) small white beans with liquid
salt and freshly ground black pepper to taste

In general, the more robust the beer, the less of it will be consumed by your guests.

Heat oven to 325°. Sauté bacon pieces in a medium skillet over medium-high heat until soft, but not crisp. With a slotted spoon, transfer bacon pieces to a plate. Add onion to skillet and cook over medium heat until soft and translucent, about 10 minutes. Place bacon, onion and remaining ingredients in a heavy baking dish and mix well. Bake uncovered for 1 hour. If beans are still quite soupy, cook for 15 to 20 additional minutes. Serve hot or warm.

STUFFED PORTOBELLO MUSHROOMS

This is delicious as a first course, or even as a luncheon or supper entrée. It takes a few minutes to scrape out the dark mushroom "gills," but it results in a more attractive dish. These can be assembled an hour or two ahead and baked just before serving. Panko crumbs are unseasoned Japanese-style dried breadcrumbs that can be found in the Asian foods section of many supermarkets.

6 portobello mushrooms, about 6 oz. each, 4-5
   inches in diameter
1 bottle (12 oz.) pale ale
6 tbs. butter
8 oz. fresh white mushrooms, trimmed,
   chopped into pea-sized pieces
2 large shallots, finely chopped
1 tbs. sherry vinegar
1 tsp. Worcestershire sauce
1 tsp. dried tarragon
salt and freshly ground pepper to taste
2-3 slices prosciutto, finely chopped, optional
⅔ cup panko or dried breadcrumbs
⅔ cup shredded Gruyère or Swiss cheese
1 tbs. milk or water, optional

Avoid using a frosted mug to serve beer. It may be fine for root beer and even a simple North American lager for quenching your thirst, but a glass that's too cold will reduce the complexity and character of a good beer's taste.

Twist off portobello mushroom stems and reserve. With a teaspoon, gently scrape out dark mushroom "gills" from the underside of mushroom caps and discard. In a large skillet, place mushrooms cap-side down in a single layer and pour in ale. Bring to a boil over high heat. Reduce heat to low, cover and simmer for 12 to 15 minutes, turning mushrooms over once during cooking. Start checking for doneness after 10 minutes. When mushrooms are tender, but still slightly firm when pierced with the tip of a sharp knife, remove from cooking liquid. Discard liquid. Line a rimmed baking sheet with aluminum foil. Place cooked mushrooms cap-side down on foil. Cut off tough ends from mushroom stems and remove a small layer of the woody outside peel. If the center parts are tender, chop into pea-sized pieces and add to chopped mushrooms for stuffing. If entire stem seems woody, discard.

Heat oven to 400°. Melt butter in a large skillet over high heat. Add chopped mushrooms and sauté for 2 to 3 minutes, until mushrooms release some liquid. Add shallots, vinegar and Worcestershire and cook for 2 to 3 minutes. Remove from heat, stir in tarragon and season with salt and pepper. Add prosciutto, panko and cheese, mixing well. Stir in milk or water if mixture needs more moisture. Mound mixture evenly inside mushroom caps. Press down lightly on stuffing. Bake for 15 minutes, until heated through and top is lightly toasted. If stuffing mixture has cooled, add 5 to 10 minutes to baking time. Serve immediately.

MUSHROOM-BEER RISOTTO

Beer accents the earthy mushroom flavors of this flavorful risotto. Italian Arborio or another short-grained rice is important for a creamy texture. This dish will also serve 4 as an entrée, or 6 to 8 as an appetizer.

1 bottle (12 oz.) lager or pale ale
1/4 oz. (about 1/3 cup) dried porcini mushrooms
1 can (14 1/2 oz.) beef broth
1 cup water
2 tbs. butter
2 tbs. olive oil
1/2 cup finely chopped onion
3-4 medium cremini or brown mushrooms, coarsely chopped
1 1/2 cups Arborio or Silver Pearl rice
1/2 tsp. fresh thyme leaves, or 1/4 tsp. dried
1/3 cup coarsely chopped *Oven-Dried Tomatoes*, page 68, or sun-dried tomatoes
2 cloves garlic, finely chopped
salt and freshly ground pepper to taste
3 tbs. finely chopped fresh parsley
1/2 cup grated Parmesan cheese

Heat beer in a small saucepan until it just boils. Remove from heat and add dried mushrooms. Let sit for 20 to 30 minutes to soften. Drain mushrooms, reserving soaking liquid. Rinse soaked mushrooms under running water to remove any remaining sand or grit. Dry on paper towels and chop coarsely. Carefully pour mushroom soaking liquid through a paper towel or coffee filter and place strained liquid in a saucepan with beef broth and water. Bring to a boil over high heat. Reduce heat to low and keep at a low simmer.

Heat butter and oil in a heavy 2- to 3-quart saucepan and sauté onion over medium heat for 5 to 6 minutes, until soft. Add fresh mushrooms and cook for 1 minute. Add rice and stir to coat with butter and oil until rice starts to turn translucent. Add thyme and dried mushrooms. Ladle in about 1 cup of the broth mixture and cook over medium heat, stirring constantly, until broth is absorbed. Continue to add boiling broth about ½ cup each time, stirring until rice has absorbed broth before adding more. Rice should remain at a simmer. Cooking over high heat does not shorten cooking time. After rice has cooked for 15 minutes, bite into a grain of rice. It should be almost cooked through with just a small hard center. Add *Oven-Dried Tomatoes*, garlic, salt and pepper. Continue to cook and stir for about 5 minutes. Stir in parsley and Parmesan cheese. Serve immediately in a heated serving bowl or on warm plates.

NOTE: A small amount of broth mixture may be left over after rice is perfectly cooked.

OVEN-DRIED TOMATOES

*These intensely flavored tomatoes keep in refrigerator for 3 to 4 days. Their bold flavor makes them a good addition to dishes cooked with beer, such as **Mushroom-Beer Risotto**, page 66.*

2-3 plum tomatoes, cored, cut lengthwise into eighths, seeds removed
salt and pepper

Heat oven to 250°. Line a baking sheet with foil or parchment paper. Place tomato pieces on sheet and sprinkle with salt and pepper. Bake for about 2 hours, until tomatoes have lost most of their moisture, but are still soft and pliable.

No steam is used in brewing "steam" beer. The process of making steam beer was developed out of necessity in San Francisco during the Gold Rush. It is made in shallow tanks and fermented with lager yeast, but at higher ale-fermenting temperatures. "Steam" is now a trademark of San Francisco's Anchor Brewing Company. Other beers made in this style are now called "California Common Beer."

ALMOND AND DRIED CHERRY PILAF

Servings: 4

Serve this almond- and fruit-studded rice pilaf with grilled meats, roasted chicken or fish. For a delicious variation, substitute dried cranberries or currants for the cherries, or pine nuts for the almonds. This dish can sit covered for up to 20 minutes before serving.

2 tbs. butter
½ cup finely chopped onion
2 whole cloves
1 cup converted rice
1 can (14½ oz.) chicken broth

½ cup pale ale or light-style lager
salt and freshly ground pepper to taste
¼ cup dried cherries or golden raisins, coarsely chopped
¼ cup toasted slivered almonds

Melt butter in a heavy medium saucepan. Sauté onion and cloves over medium heat for 4 to 5 minutes, until onion softens. Add rice, stir to coat with butter and cook until rice turns milky and translucent. Add chicken broth, ale, salt, pepper and dried fruit. Bring to a boil over high heat. Reduce heat to very low, cover and cook for 20 to 25 minutes, until rice is tender and liquid has been absorbed. Remove cloves and discard. Add almonds and fluff rice with a fork. Remove cloves and discard. Serve warm.

SWEET POTATO AND APPLE CASSEROLE WITH HONEY WHEAT BEER

Servings: 6

This slightly sweet dish goes together quickly if you have cooked fresh or well-drained canned sweet potatoes. It is a delicious accompaniment for roasted pork, turkey or ham.

2-3 Golden Delicious or other cooking apples, peeled, cored
3-4 small sweet potatoes, cooked, peeled
1/3 cup brown sugar, packed
1/4 cup butter

1/2 cup honey wheat beer
1/2 tsp. finely grated peeled ginger root
1 tbs. lemon juice
1/2 tsp. cinnamon
generous amount freshly grated nutmeg
salt and freshly ground pepper to taste

Heat oven to 325°. Cut apples into quarters; cut each quarter into 1/4-inch-thick slices. Cut sweet potatoes into 1/2-inch-thick pieces about the same size as apples. Lightly butter a medium-sized ovenproof serving dish or casserole. Alternate layers of sweet potatoes and apples until all are used. In a small saucepan, combine remaining ingredients. Bring to a boil over high heat. Reduce heat to low and simmer for 3 to 4 minutes, until sugar dissolves. Pour hot liquid over sweet potatoes and apples. Bake uncovered for 25 to 30 minutes, until apples are soft. Baste once or twice during baking by spooning liquid from bottom of casserole over the top. Serve hot.

POTATO GRATIN

Serve this creamy potato dish with grilled or roasted meats. Soaking the potato slices makes them easy to separate and layer into the baking pan and prevents them from turning brown. Use the food processor's 2 mm. slicing blade for the potatoes. For a variation, sauté 1 large onion or leek in butter and layer between potatoes. Or, add 1 cup coarsely shredded Gruyère or Swiss cheese between potato layers.

1 clove garlic, cut in half
2 tbs. butter
2 lb. russet potatoes

salt and freshly ground pepper to taste
¾ cup heavy cream
1 cup chicken broth

Rub cut side of garlic clove over a deep-sided 10-inch baking dish. Generously butter the bottom and sides of dish and set aside. Peel potatoes and slice about ⅛-inch thick. Place potatoes in a large bowl, cover with cold water and soak for 30 minutes. Change water 2 to 3 times to rinse off most of the surface starch. Drain potatoes and pat dry.

Heat oven to 375°. Arrange potatoes in layers in baking dish, sprinkling every other layer with salt and pepper. In a small saucepan, heat cream and chicken broth together until hot to touch; do not boil. Pour mixture over potatoes. Dot top of potatoes with any remaining butter. Bake uncovered for 50 to 60 minutes, until potatoes are tender and top is nicely browned.

BEER WITH BRUNCH AND SUPPER DISHES

PAIRING BRUNCH AND SUPPER DISHES WITH BEER

Here is a collection of familiar and comforting any-time-of-day dishes. *Beer Pancakes* are a classic recipe. The beer gives them a wonderful light puffy texture, and maple syrup echoes some of the beer flavors. *Cornmeal Waffles* are also delicious teamed with maple syrup, topped with savory creamed chicken or tuna, or made into a special appetizer with smoked salmon. Make *Savory Cheese and Bread Pudding* for a company breakfast or brunch.

Beer and cheese are very complementary and it is easy to make some delicious matches. *Beer Fondue* is a spicy one, using hot pepper cheese. Use tortilla chips rather than French bread cubes for dipping, and drink your favorite Mexican or wheat beer, or even an Octoberfest or celebration ale. *Welsh Rabbit* is a popular English dish usually served over toast for supper. It goes well with Scotch or dark amber ales and, in smaller portions, makes a delicious, informal cheese course.

The phrase "mind your Ps and Qs" dates back to the days of old in England. Tavern keepers used this phrase to remind their barmaids to keep track of how many pints or quarts of beer they delivered to each patron.

BUTTERMILK-ALE PANCAKES

Makes fifteen 5-inch pancakes

These light pancakes make a delicious main attraction for breakfast, brunch or supper. If you have any leftovers, cover them with plastic wrap and refrigerate. For a quick breakfast, drizzle with syrup and heat for a minute or two in the microwave.

1 egg
1/4 cup vegetable oil or melted butter
1/2 tsp. salt
2 tsp. honey
1 cup pale ale
1 cup buttermilk

2 cups flour
1 tsp. baking powder
2 tsp. baking soda
butter, optional
warmed maple syrup, optional
raspberry jam, optional

Whisk egg, oil, salt and honey together in a large bowl. Stir in ale and buttermilk. Sift together flour, baking powder and baking soda. Gradually add flour mixture to buttermilk mixture, stirring just until dry ingredients are moistened. Heat a griddle or heavy skillet to medium-high and grease lightly with oil or nonstick cooking spray. Spoon about 3 tbs. batter for each pancake onto griddle. Cook until a few bubbles appear on top. Turn pancakes over and cook for 1 to 2 additional minutes, until bottom is lightly browned. Transfer to a warm plate. Keep pancakes warm while cooking remaining batter. Serve on heated plates. Pass butter and warmed maple syrup, or spread pancakes with raspberry jam.

CORNMEAL BEER WAFFLES

These waffles make a delicious weekend breakfast treat. Or, serve them for brunch or supper with a creamed green chile and chicken or tuna topping.

½ cup buttermilk
¼ cup vegetable oil
2 eggs
½ tsp. salt
1 tbs. sugar

½ cup light-bodied lager or ale
¾ cup flour
½ cup cornmeal
1 tsp. baking powder
1 tsp. baking soda

Heat a waffle iron and spray grids with nonstick cooking spray. In a bowl, whisk together buttermilk, oil, eggs, salt and sugar until well combined. Add beer and stir gently. In a small bowl, combine flour, cornmeal, baking powder and soda and stir well. Whisk flour mixture into egg mixture just until flour is incorporated. Fill waffle iron with batter and bake according to manufacturer's directions until golden brown. Serve immediately.

VARIATION: SMOKED SALMON ON CORNMEAL BEER WAFFLES

Spread hot waffles with a thin layer of sour cream and top with thinly sliced smoked salmon. Cut into bite-sized pieces and serve as an appetizer.

QUICK PEPPERONI PIZZA

Beer and pizza make a delicious twosome. If you are short on time, use a prepared pizza crust from the supermarket and use purchased pizza sauce and well-drained canned mushrooms. Drink a pilsner or dark lager.

4 plum tomatoes, sliced ¼-inch-thick, seeds removed
salt and freshly ground pepper to taste
6 fresh mushrooms, trimmed, cut into ¼-inch slices
Easy Pizza Crust, pages 138-139

¾ cup coarsely shredded mozzarella cheese
1 tsp. dried oregano
2-3 oz. thinly sliced pepperoni
2-3 tbs. grated Parmesan cheese
dash red pepper flakes

Heat oven to 475° with a pizza stone if desired. Line a microwave-safe plate with a double layer of paper towels. Place sliced tomatoes on towels, sprinkle with salt and pepper and cook on HIGH for 1½ minutes. Let stand for 5 minutes and blot dry. Using fresh paper towels, cook sliced mushrooms in the same manner as tomatoes.

Roll pizza dough on a work surface to a 13- to 14-inch circle. Spread mozzarella cheese evenly over dough and sprinkle with oregano. Arrange pepperoni pieces over cheese and top with tomatoes and mushrooms. Sprinkle with Parmesan cheese and red pepper flakes. Bake on pizza stone, or a baking sheet on the lowest oven rack, for about 15 to 20 minutes, until nicely browned and bubbling. Serve hot.

BEER FONDUE

This beer and cheese fondue has a south-of-the-border twist. Use Mexican beer in the fondue and to drink with it. Celery sticks, carrot sticks and blanched cauliflower or broccoli florets also make delicious dippers. Provide a small plate and a long-handled fork for each person for spearing bread cubes and/or vegetables.

¾ cup light-bodied Mexican beer, such as Corona or
   Carta Blanca 6 oz → 2x = 1 bottle
1 cup shredded sharp cheddar cheese
1 cup shredded pepper Jack cheese
tortilla chips or French bread cubes for dipping

Pour beer into a heavy saucepan or fondue pot and heat gently over medium-low heat. Gradually add cheeses and stir continuously until melted. If not using a fondue pot, pour mixture into a small heavy casserole and keep warm over a candle or low flame. Serve with tortilla chips or French bread cubes.

National beer production from commercial American brewers first reached one million barrels in 1860. By 1867, it had increased to six million.

WELSH RABBIT

This dish, also commonly called Welsh Rarebit, consists of cheese melted with seasonings and served over toast. It makes a comforting, easy supper. This dish was supposedly so-named because it was served in place of the hoped-for game after an unsuccessful afternoon of hunting.

1 tbs. butter
1/4 cup porter or stout
1/2 tsp. dry mustard
freshly ground pepper to taste
1/2 tsp. Worcestershire sauce
3-4 drops Tabasco Sauce
1 1/2 cups shredded cheddar
    cheese
4 slices toasted bread

Until a century and a half ago, almost all beers were cloudy, if not murky. They were commonly served in opaque pottery, wood or pewter tankards, some fitted with lids to keep out flies and other flying insects.

Melt butter in a medium saucepan. Add porter, mustard, pepper, Worcestershire and Tabasco and heat over medium-high heat until almost boiling. Reduce heat to low and add cheese, stirring just enough to melt cheese. Do not let mixture boil after adding cheese. Serve immediately on warm plates over hot toasted bread. Or, place toasted bread on ovenproof plates, top with cheese mixture and place under the broiler until lightly browned.

SAVORY CHEESE AND BREAD PUDDING

This substantial brunch or supper dish can be made a day ahead.

2 tbs. butter
1 large onion, finely chopped
8 oz. white mushrooms, thinly sliced
1/2 tsp. dried tarragon
dash red pepper flakes
6-7 cups firm bread cubes, 1-inch cubes
4 thin slices ham, cut into about 1-inch
  squares

1½ cups shredded Gruyère or Gouda
  cheese
1⅔ cups half-and-half
1/3 cup amber or pale ale
4 eggs
1 tsp. Worcestershire sauce
1 tsp. Dijon mustard
salt and freshly ground pepper to taste

Heat butter in a large skillet over low heat and sauté onion for 6 to 8 minutes, until softened. Increase heat to high and add mushrooms, tarragon and red pepper flakes. Cook, stirring, for 4 to 5 minutes, until mushrooms have released their liquid and are lightly browned. Butter an 8-x-10-inch baking pan or 12-inch gratin dish and add bread cubes. Top with mushroom mixture, ham pieces and shredded cheese. Whisk together half-and-half, ale, eggs, Worcestershire, mustard, salt and pepper. Pour mixture over bread and press down with a spoon to moisten bread. Refrigerate for at least 30 minutes or overnight. Heat oven to 375°. Bake for 30 to 35 minutes, until puffed. Let rest for 10 minutes before serving. If refrigerated for more than 4 hours, add 10 to 15 minutes to baking time.

BEER WITH POULTRY

PAIRING POULTRY WITH BEER

Poultry is a very popular choice for today's entrées, since it cooks quickly and is low in fat. Versatile poultry does well in dishes using a variety of spices, vegetable accompaniments and cooking methods. Beer adds a delicious flavor component to poultry when used in sauces and marinades.

Chicken Jambalaya, Quick Chicken Stir-Fry with Pasta, Turkey Chile Verde and *Grilled Chicken Soft Tacos* are perfect beer food and will stand up to full-bodied brews. Beer gives a delicious flavor to *Ale-Roasted Chicken with Carrots* and *Chicken Breasts with Mushroom-Stout Sauce. Turkey Mushroom Meatballs* can be served as a party appetizer or main course. *Curried Cornish Game Hens* are delicious hot or cold and make delicious picnic food. The curry rub works well for roasted chicken, too. There are many appetizing ways to pair beer and poultry. These recipes are just a starting point.

 *In the 1600s, each crew member on New England sailing ships was entitled to one quart of beer per day. The Mayflower is said to have landed at Plymouth Rock instead of Virginia, as intended, because provisions, especially beer, were running low.*

GRILLED CHICKEN SOFT TACOS

Boneless, skinless chicken thighs or breasts are marinated then quickly grilled to provide a smoky flavor to this authentic Mexican taco. Drink a Mexican brew, such as Dos Equis or Negra Modelo, to keep in the spirit. Top with a little guacamole and sour cream if you like.

1 lb. boneless, skinless chicken thighs
   or breasts
2 tbs. fresh lime juice
2 tbs. vegetable oil
1 tsp. chili powder
salt and freshly ground pepper to taste

1 can (15 oz.) black beans
8 corn tortillas, warmed
Spicy Salsa, page 83, or your favorite
   prepared hot or mild fresh salsa
1 cup shredded cheddar cheese
fresh cilantro leaves for garnish

Flatten chicken pieces or cut to a uniform thickness. In a bowl, combine lime juice, vegetable oil, $\frac{1}{2}$ tsp. of the chili powder, salt and pepper. Add chicken pieces and toss to coat well. Marinate for 30 minutes in the refrigerator. Grill over high heat until nicely browned and juices run clear. Slice cooked chicken into $\frac{1}{2}$-inch strips just before assembling tacos. Heat beans in a small saucepan with remaining $\frac{1}{2}$ tsp. chili powder. Lift beans out with a slotted spoon and place in a serving bowl. For each taco, place a warm tortilla on a serving plate. Top with a few chicken slices, 1 to 2 spoonfuls of beans, and a small amount of salsa, cheese and cilantro. Fold up to eat.

SPICY SALSA

This tomato-based salsa is delicious on tacos, quesadillas and hamburgers, or with chips. Add salt and pepper just before serving; otherwise, the tomatoes tend to release too much juice.

4 large ripe tomatoes, peeled, seeded, chopped
1 large ripe avocado, diced
4-5 green onions, white part only, finely chopped
2 jalapeño chiles, seeded, finely chopped
½ tsp. dried oregano
1 tbs. fresh lime juice
½ tsp. sugar
¼ cup chopped fresh cilantro
salt and freshly ground pepper to taste

Combine ingredients in a small nonmetallic bowl and refrigerate for about 30 minutes before serving.

Many mass-produced North American lagers are "heavy brewed." They are brewed to have a high alcohol, malt and hop content; then, they are diluted to the desired strength, and carbonated just before bottling. This method increases brewing capacity by as much as 30 percent with little added equipment.

CHICKEN BREASTS WITH MUSHROOM-STOUT SAUCE

Boneless chicken breasts make a quick dinner. Brown or cremini mushrooms have great flavor if you can find them. Serve this dish with creamy polenta, mashed potatoes or steamed rice. Drink more oatmeal stout, porter or amber ale.

4 boneless, skinless chicken breasts
salt and pepper
flour for dusting
3 tbs. olive oil
2 tbs. finely chopped shallots
8 oz. small mushrooms, trimmed, thinly sliced
1 cup chicken broth
½ cup oatmeal stout or porter
1 tsp. Worcestershire sauce
½ tsp. dried tarragon
1 tbs. flour
salt and freshly ground pepper to taste
2-3 tbs. finely chopped fresh parsley

 *Inexpensive clear beer glasses were first produced in America in the early 1800s, replacing pewter, wood, clay and even leather tankards.*

Flatten chicken breasts between sheets of plastic wrap to a thickness of about 3/8 inch. Season with salt and pepper and dust lightly with flour. Add olive oil to a heated skillet and sauté chicken breasts over medium heat for about 2 to 3 minutes on each side, until lightly browned. Transfer to a plate and cover with foil. Add shallots to skillet and cook for 1 minute until softened, but not brown. Add mushrooms, increase heat to high and sauté for 4 to 5 minutes, until most of the liquid is released from the mushrooms. Place chicken broth, stout, Worcestershire and tarragon in a small saucepan and bring to a boil. Stir 1 tbs. flour into mushroom mixture and cook for 1 to 2 minutes. Add boiling broth mixture to mushroom mixture and stir until thickened. Taste for seasoning, adding salt and pepper if needed. Return chicken breasts to pan and top with sauce. Reduce heat to low, cover pan and cook for 10 to 15 minutes, turning chicken over once. Sprinkle with parsley and serve immediately.

CHICKEN JAMBALAYA

Servings: 4-6

Use spicy smoked Cajun andouille sausage if you can find it. Polish sausage is a good substitute, but precook it to get rid of some of the excess fat. Serve with a porter, bock or your favorite lager.

3 tbs. olive oil
8 boneless chicken thighs, skin removed, cut in half
2 medium onions, chopped
½ cup diced celery
1½ cups diced red, green and/or yellow bell peppers
2 large cloves garlic, finely chopped
1 tsp. chili powder
1 tsp. dried basil
1½ cups uncooked rice
1 cup diced full-flavored ham
½ lb. andouille sausage, thinly sliced
1 can (14½ oz.) ready-cut tomatoes with juice
2½-3 cups chicken broth
½ tsp. Tabasco Sauce
salt and freshly ground pepper to taste
¼ cup finely chopped fresh parsley

In the United States, a pint is one-eighth of a U.S. gallon, or 16 fluid ounces. In England, a pint is one-eighth of an Imperial gallon, or 20 fluid ounces. Half-pint glasses are usually called schooners.

Heat oven to 350°. Heat olive oil over medium-high heat in a heavy ovenproof Dutch oven and brown chicken on both sides; transfer to a plate. Add onions, celery and peppers to Dutch oven and sauté over medium heat for 10 minutes. Add garlic, chili powder and basil and cook for another minute. Stir in rice and cook for 3 to 4 minutes, until rice turns translucent. Push rice to one side and return chicken to Dutch oven. Spoon rice over chicken and add ham, sausage, tomatoes, 2½ cups chicken broth, Tabasco, salt and pepper. Bring to a boil on the stovetop, cover tightly and bake in oven for about 45 to 50 minutes, until rice is tender. Stir rice once or twice during baking and check to see if there is enough liquid. Add a small amount of chicken broth or water if needed. Sprinkle with parsley and serve hot.

QUICK CHICKEN STIR-FRY WITH PASTA

Servings: 4

The sauce cooks in about the same amount of time it takes to bring the pasta water to a boil and cook the pasta. Use oreccheiette (little ears), radiatore (little radiators), fusilli (small spirals) or another shape of pasta that will catch the tasty sauce. Serve with an Irish lager, amber ale or oatmeal stout.

5-6 qt. water
1 lb. boneless, skinless chicken thighs
   or breasts
3 tbs. olive oil
$\frac{1}{2}$ tsp. red pepper flakes, or more to
   taste
1 cup diced onion
3 cloves garlic, finely chopped
12 oz. white mushrooms, trimmed,
   thinly sliced
1 cup chicken broth

2 tbs. tomato paste
1 small red bell pepper, seeded, cut
   into thin strips
2 tsp. salt
8 oz. dry pasta
1 cup loosely packed fresh basil leaves,
   cut into thin ribbons
1 cup peeled, seeded, chopped fresh
   tomatoes
grated Parmesan cheese
salt and freshly ground pepper to taste

Heat water over high heat in a large pot until boiling.

While water is heating, cut chicken into about 5/8-inch cubes. Heat olive oil in a large skillet over high heat. Add red pepper flakes and chicken pieces. Stir-fry chicken for 3 to 4 minutes, until lightly browned; transfer to a plate with a slotted spoon. Add onion to skillet and stir-fry for 1 to 2 minutes, until softened. Add garlic and mushrooms and stir-fry for about 4 to 5 minutes, until mushrooms are lightly browned and liquid has been released. Add chicken broth and tomato paste to skillet and stir well to combine. Add red peppers and return chicken to skillet. Reduce heat to medium-low, until liquid is simmering rapidly.

When water is at a rolling boil, add 2 tsp. salt and pasta. Stir during the first minute to keep pasta from sticking together. Bite into a piece of pasta 1 to 2 minutes before the cooking time indicated on the pasta package has elapsed. When pasta is barely cooked through, *al dente*, drain in a colander, but do not rinse. Immediately pour drained pasta into skillet with chicken mixture and stir to combine. Continue to cook for 1 to 2 minutes, until pasta absorbs some of the sauce. Add basil and tomato pieces and a generous sprinkle of Parmesan cheese. Season with salt and pepper and toss to combine. Serve immediately in a heated serving bowl or place directly on heated plates. Pass more cheese and red pepper flakes.

ROASTED CHICKEN WITH MAPLE PORTER GARLIC-GINGER SAUCE

Servings: 3-4

Spoon this mildly spicy sauce over carved roasted chicken pieces. Creamy mashed potatoes or hot rice make a good side dish. Substitute brown ale if maple porter isn't available and drink a pilsner, brown ale or oatmeal stout.

1 frying chicken, about 4 lb., rinsed, dried
salt
2 quarter-sized pieces ginger root, unpeeled
4 cloves garlic, smashed

SAUCE
1 tsp. finely chopped unpeeled ginger root
1 large clove garlic, finely chopped
1 bottle (12 oz.) maple porter
2 tbs. currant jelly
¼ tsp. red pepper flakes
2 tsp. cornstarch
1 tbs. cold water
salt and freshly ground pepper to taste

Before tankards and glasses, ancient civilizations (Babylonians, Egyptians, Greeks, et al.) drank from a large vessel with straws or tubes. Royalty had straws made of gold.

Heat oven to 375°. Lightly sprinkle inside of chicken with salt; add ginger and garlic cloves to cavity. Place chicken on a rack in a roasting pan and roast for 1 to 1¼ hours, until a thermometer reads 185° when inserted into the thickest part of the thigh and the juices run clear when thigh is pierced.

For sauce, combine chopped ginger, garlic, beer, jelly and hot pepper flakes in a small saucepan. Bring to a boil over high heat. Reduce heat to low and simmer for 5 minutes.

About 15 minutes before chicken is done, brush with a small amount of sauce. Transfer chicken to a plate and let stand for 10 minutes before carving. Strain sauce into a saucepan and bring to a boil. Dissolve cornstarch in water and add to sauce. Cook, stirring, until sauce thickens. Season with salt and pepper. Serve hot sauce over carved chicken pieces.

ALE-ROASTED CHICKEN WITH CARROTS

The carrots, onions and garlic in this recipe cook in the bottom of the roasting pan and soak up the flavorful basting sauce. Serve with a brown ale or bock, a green salad and some crunchy garlic bread for a satisfying cool-weather supper.

1 frying chicken, about 4 lb., rinsed, dried
salt
2 cups water, plus more if needed
1 lb. carrots, trimmed
3-4 small onions, cut into quarters

6-8 large cloves garlic
½ cup amber ale
2 tbs. butter, melted
1 tbs. Worcestershire sauce
½ tsp. finely grated peeled ginger root

Heat oven to 400°. Season inside of chicken with salt and place on a roasting rack in a large roasting pan with water. Leave carrots whole if they are less than 1 inch in diameter; cut thicker carrots in half. Place carrots, onions and garlic in roasting pan. Roast for about 1 to 1¼ hours, until a thermometer reads 185° when inserted into the thickest part of the thigh and the juices run clear when thigh is pierced. Combine remaining ingredients and brush over chicken every 15 minutes while roasting. Stir vegetables once during roasting and add a small amount of water if pan seems dry. About 15 minutes before chicken is done, pour remaining ale mixture over chicken. Let chicken rest for a few minutes before carving. Strain liquid from pan into a cup and skim off fat. Pour into a small pitcher and pass with carved chicken and vegetables.

BEER-BRAISED CHICKEN THIGHS

This tender chicken dish can be made a day before serving. Accompany with buttered noodles or boiled potatoes and some cooked peas or green beans. Drink a brown or Scotch ale.

8 chicken thighs, skin removed
salt and pepper
flour for dusting
1 tbs. butter
1 tbs. olive oil
1/4 cup finely chopped shallots
1/2 cup porter or other dark beer

1/2 cup chicken broth
1 tbs. lemon juice
1/2 tsp. dried tarragon
1/3 cup heavy cream
salt and freshly ground pepper to taste
2 tbs. finely chopped fresh parsley

Season chicken with salt and pepper and dust with flour; shake off excess. Heat butter and oil in a heavy skillet over medium-high heat and brown chicken on all sides. Do not allow butter to burn. Reduce heat to medium, add shallots and cook for 3 to 4 minutes, until shallots are soft. Add beer, chicken broth, lemon juice and tarragon and bring to a boil. Reduce heat to low, cover pan and simmer for 10 minutes. Transfer chicken to a plate. Increase heat to high and cook sauce until reduced by about half. Stir in cream and return chicken to pan. Simmer uncovered for 15 to 20 minutes, until chicken is tender. Taste, adjust seasonings and garnish with parsley.

SPICY BRAISED CHICKEN LEGS

Servings: 3-4

Chicken pieces are braised in an aromatic lager marinade and finished under the broiler to form a hoisin-sesame crust. Drumsticks done this way make terrific finger food for a party. These can be made a day ahead, refrigerated and reheated just before serving. Drink a brown ale or Chinese beer, such as Tsing Tao.

8 chicken thighs or 10 drumsticks
1 orange
1 cup American lager
1 cup water
¼ cup soy sauce
2 tbs. honey
2 tbs. cider vinegar
2 cloves garlic, thinly sliced
3 quarter-sized pieces ginger root
2 whole star anise, or 1 tsp. fennel seeds
2 tsp. red pepper flakes
2 tbs. hoisin sauce
2 tsp. sesame oil

In China, beer is easier to find and cheaper to buy than bottled water.

Remove skin and fat from chicken. If using drumsticks, make a circular cut through the tendon with a knife all the way to the bone, starting about 1 inch from the small end of drumstick. Remove the tough cartilage below the knife cut and discard. This will encourage the meat to contract into a compact piece during cooking. Rinse chicken and pat dry.

With a vegetable peeler, remove zest from orange in large strips. Squeeze juice from orange and combine with peel, beer, water, soy sauce, honey, vinegar, garlic, ginger root, star anise and red pepper flakes in a medium skillet with a tight-fitting lid that is large enough to hold chicken pieces in a single layer. Bring mixture to a boil over high heat. Reduce heat to low and simmer for 15 minutes. Add chicken pieces to skillet, cover and simmer for 20 to 25 minutes, until chicken is quite tender. Turn chicken over once during cooking. Remove lid and cool chicken in braising liquid for 20 minutes. Drain chicken and discard liquid. Refrigerate chicken if not eating immediately.

Just before serving, heat broiler. Combine hoisin sauce and sesame oil and brush on both sides of chicken pieces. Place chicken on a rack in a roasting pan and place in oven about 6 inches from heat source. Broil for 3 to 4 minutes on each side, until chicken is nicely glazed and heated through.

CURRIED CORNISH GAME HENS

*A fragrant garlic and spice mixture stuffed under the skin bastes the game hens while roasting. Serve with **Almond and Dried Cherry Pilaf**, page 69, and drink a Thai beer, such as Singha, or amber ale. These birds are also delicious cold and make great picnic fare.*

1 tbs. vegetable oil
3 cloves garlic, thinly sliced
1 tsp. finely chopped peeled ginger root
pinch red pepper flakes
2 tsp. curry powder
1/8 tsp. cinnamon
1/8 tsp. ground coriander
2 Cornish game hens, about 1 1/4 lb. each
4 whole cloves garlic
salt and freshly ground pepper to taste
1/4 cup amber ale
1/4 cup chicken broth
1 tsp. brown sugar

During the early colonial days, employees expected beer breaks as part of their employment benefits. This had been the custom in England.

Heat oven to 425°. Heat 2 tsp. of the vegetable oil in a small skillet over low heat. Add sliced garlic, ginger and red pepper flakes and sauté for 1 to 2 minutes to soften garlic. Stir in curry powder, cinnamon and coriander and cook for another minute, until the aroma from the spices is released. Remove from heat and cool for 10 minutes.

Rinse and pat dry game hens. Starting at the top of the breastbone, carefully loosen the skin over breasts with your fingers, making a pocket. Spoon a small amount of garlic and curry mixture under skin of each hen, distributing spices over breast and thigh meat as far as possible. Place 2 of the garlic cloves inside each bird and tie legs closed with kitchen string. Rub skin with remaining oil and sprinkle each hen with salt and pepper. Place hens on a rack in a roasting pan and roast for 40 to 50 minutes, until a thermometer reads 175° when the thickest part of a thigh is pierced.

While hens are roasting, combine ale, chicken broth and brown sugar in same skillet used for spice mixture and bring to a boil over high heat. Boil for 2 minutes and remove from heat. Baste hens with ale mixture every 10 to 15 minutes. When hens are done, remove from oven and let stand for 10 to 15 minutes before serving. To serve 4, use kitchen scissors or a carving knife to cut birds in half.

TURKEY MUSHROOM MEATBALLS

Makes 36

Serve these with mashed potatoes or polenta to catch the rich beer sauce. Drink a bock or amber ale. Use the food processor to chop the mushrooms. You can also make these into smaller cocktail-sized meatballs and serve with toothpicks for a party.

½ cup fresh breadcrumbs, crusts
    removed
½ cup milk
7 tbs. butter
4 green onions, white part only, finely
    chopped
4 oz. white mushrooms, stemmed,
    finely chopped
2 cloves garlic, finely chopped
1 lb. ground turkey
1 egg, lightly beaten

½ tsp. dried thyme
½ tsp. dry mustard
freshly grated nutmeg to taste
salt and freshly ground pepper to taste
2 tbs. finely chopped fresh parsley
3 tbs. flour
1¼ cups chicken broth
1¼ cups amber ale or American lager
2 tbs. soy sauce
2 tbs. tomato paste

Combine breadcrumbs with milk in a small bowl; set aside. Heat 2 tbs. of the butter in a large skillet over medium heat. Add onions, mushrooms and garlic and sauté until moisture has cooked out of mushroom mixture. Remove from heat. Squeeze milk from breadcrumbs and discard milk. Add soaked breadcrumbs to mushroom mixture and mix well. Cool. In a large bowl, combine ground turkey, egg, thyme, mustard, nutmeg, salt, pepper and parsley. Add cooled mushroom mixture and mix well. Form mixture into ¾-inch balls.

Wipe out skillet, add 2 tbs. of the butter and melt over medium heat. Sauté a few meatballs at a time in butter until lightly browned on all sides; transfer to a plate. When all meatballs are browned, add remaining 3 tbs. butter and flour to skillet. Scrape up browned bits from the bottom of pan and pour in chicken broth, beer, soy sauce and tomato paste. Slowly bring mixture to a boil, stirring constantly. Adjust seasonings. Return meatballs to pan, cover and simmer for 20 minutes over low heat. Serve hot.

 *Robust, full-flavored foods need dark, full-bodied beers as accompaniments to stand up to the foods' strong flavors.*

TURKEY CHILI VERDE

Turkey chunks are cooked with tomatillos, white beans and spicy jalapeños in this savory stew. Serve with hot tortillas and your favorite Mexican brew.

2 tbs. vegetable oil
2 large onions, finely chopped
4 large cloves garlic, finely chopped
3-4 jalapeño chiles, seeded,
    finely chopped
2 tbs. ground cumin
1 tsp. dried oregano
1 lb. turkey tenderloins or breast
    pieces, cut into ⅜-inch cubes

1 can (7 oz.) whole roasted green
    chiles, drained, seeded, chopped
1 can (12 oz.) whole tomatillos with
    juice, coarsely chopped
2 cans (14½ oz. each) chicken broth
1 cup light Mexican beer, such as Corona
1 tsp. salt
2 cans (15 oz. each) small white beans
¼ cup coarsely chopped fresh cilantro

Heat vegetable oil in a heavy stockpot. Sauté onions over medium-low heat for 8 to 10 minutes, until softened. Add garlic, jalapeños, cumin and oregano and cook for 1 to 2 minutes. Add turkey, green chiles, tomatillos, chicken broth, beer and salt and bring to a boil. Reduce heat, partially cover and simmer for 25 minutes. Puree 1 can of beans and their liquid with a food processor or blender. Drain remaining can of beans. Add pureed and whole beans to stockpot and heat through. Garnish with cilantro and serve in soup bowls.

BEER WITH MEAT DISHES

PAIRING MEAT DISHES WITH BEER

Beer can be a major flavor component in hearty meat stews and casseroles, adding complexity to the cooking liquid. Beer contains a natural acidity, a slight bitterness from the hops, and sometimes a slight tinge of malty sweetness, which enhances caramelized onions, carrots and browned meat juices. We have included several classic stew-type recipes, including *Carbonnade a la Flammande* and *Beer-Braised Spareribs*. *Choucroute Garnie*, while made with white wine, calls for beer as an accompaniment for the spicy cabbage and rich sausages. Curries, chilis and grilled meats all accept beer as an ingredient as well as an accompanying beverage.

Amber ales, pale ales, honey porters and dark lagers are used to make flavorful creamy brown sauces for pork dishes, sometimes accented with capers or dried fruits. Try *Pork Chops Stuffed with Apples and Dried Cherries* or *Ham with Apricot Ale Sauce*. *Roasted Pork with Brown Ale Sauce* makes an excellent company dinner and the leftovers make tasty sandwiches. *Italian Sausage Calzones* are perfect picnic food and feature beer in the easy food-processor crust.

In general, the bitterness of beer intensifies with long cooking times and high heats. Choose milder, less-bitter types of ales and lagers for these purposes. Some honey porters are soft and flavorful without much bitter taste. Another secret to success is to use another cooking liquid along with beer so that beer accounts for only up to half of the total liquid. Chicken or beef broth pair deliciously with beer in sauces.

PORTER-BRAISED BEEF BRISKET

Servings: 8-10

Serve this slow-cooked pot roast on a cold evening with garlic mashed potatoes, buttered noodles or polenta, and some caramelized carrots. Drink a porter or brown ale. Use the leftover meat to make terrific sandwiches.

3 cups thinly sliced onions
1 beef brisket, about 4½ lb., fat trimmed
1 tsp. salt
freshly ground pepper to taste
1 tbs. Worcestershire sauce
2 tbs. tomato paste
1 tsp. dry mustard

4 large garlic cloves, smashed
1 bay leaf
1 cup porter or amber ale
¼ tsp. red pepper flakes
1 tbs. cornstarch dissolved in 2 tbs.
　　water, optional

Heat oven to 350°. Place ½ of the onions in a heavy baking dish with a tight-fitting lid. Place brisket on top and season with salt and pepper. Combine Worcestershire, tomato paste and mustard and spread over brisket. Add remaining onions, garlic, bay leaf, beer and pepper flakes. Cover tightly and bake for 3 to 3½ hours, until meat is very tender. Remove meat and slice thinly across the grain. Arrange on a serving platter with onions. Strain pan juices into a small saucepan and skim and discard as much fat as possible. For a thicker sauce, bring pan juices to a boil in a small saucepan. Add a small amount of dissolved cornstarch and cook for 2 to 3 minutes until sauce reaches desired consistency, adding more if necessary.

BEER-BRAISED SHORT RIBS

Servings: 6

This comforting recipe can be cooked on the stovetop or baked in the oven. These ribs are even better made a day ahead and refrigerated. Spoon the savory sauce over buttered noodles or mashed potatoes. Drink a brown or amber ale.

4 lb. English short ribs, separated into individual ribs
2 tbs. olive oil
1 medium onion, coarsely chopped
1 large rib celery, coarsely chopped
1 jalapeño chile, seeded, finely chopped
3 cloves garlic, thinly sliced
1 medium turnip, cut into 1-inch chunks
2 large carrots, coarsely chopped
2 cans (14½ oz. each) beef broth
1 cup American lager or pale ale
1 bay leaf
½ tsp. dried thyme
½ tsp. dry mustard
2 tbs. tomato paste
salt and freshly ground pepper to taste
hot pepper sauce to taste, optional

The first beer cans appeared in the United States in 1935, but were not widely accepted until a liner was developed to keep the beer from acquiring a metallic taste from the can. In 1969, for the first time, more canned beer than bottled beer was sold.

Heat broiler. Line a rimmed baking sheet with foil and place a roasting rack inside pan. Lightly spray rack with nonstick cooking spray. Wipe short ribs with a damp paper towel to remove any bone chips and place on rack. Broil ribs about 6 inches from heat source for 5 to 6 minutes on each side, until lightly browned. Set aside.

Add oil to a large heavy saucepan or Dutch oven with a tight-fitting lid. Add onion and sauté over medium heat until softened. Add celery and jalapeño and sauté for 3 to 4 minutes. Add garlic and cook for another minute. Place browned ribs in pan and add turnip, carrots, beef broth, beer, bay leaf, thyme, mustard and tomato paste. Bring liquid to a boil over high heat. Cover tightly, reduce heat to low and simmer gently for about 2 hours, until meat is tender.

Transfer ribs to a platter and cover with foil. Strain vegetables and cooking liquid over a saucepan, pressing hard on cooked vegetables to extract as much juice as possible. Discard vegetables. Skim and discard fat and bring liquid to a boil over high heat. Cook for about 5 to 8 minutes, until volume is reduced by about 1/3. Taste for seasoning and add salt, pepper and hot sauce, if using. Add short ribs back to sauce and heat through to serve, or cool and refrigerate.

To reheat ribs, heat on the stovetop over low heat until heated through. Or, heat oven to 350°, cover and bake for 20 to 25 minutes.

NOTE: To bake ribs in the oven, heat oven to 325°. After liquid comes to a boil, cover and bake for about 2 hours, until meat is tender.

SAUERBRATEN

Start marinating the meat 3 to 4 days in advance to get the classic piquant taste of this German dish. Serve with potato pancakes or noodles, and a brown ale or German lager.

MARINADE
1 large onion, chopped
1 carrot, chopped
1 stalk celery, chopped
2 whole cloves
1 bay leaf

5-6 peppercorns
5-6 juniper berries
1 cup dry red wine
½ cup red wine vinegar
2 cups water

2½-3 lb. eye of round or top round roast,
    well trimmed
salt and pepper
flour for dusting
¼ cup vegetable oil
½ cup finely chopped onion

½ cup finely chopped carrot
½ cup finely chopped celery
2 tbs. flour
2 tbs. tomato paste
½ cup crushed gingersnaps
salt and freshly ground pepper to taste

Combine marinade ingredients in a saucepan and bring to a boil. Remove from heat and cool to room temperature. Place roast in a large locking plastic bag or nonreactive bowl just large enough to hold meat. Add cooled marinade. Seal bag well or cover bowl securely and refrigerate for 3 to 4 days, turning meat over each day. Marinade should cover meat.

When ready to cook, remove meat from marinade. Strain marinade, reserving liquid and discarding solids. Pat meat dry. Season meat with salt and pepper and dust with flour. Heat oil over high heat in a large heavy Dutch oven and brown meat well on all sides. Transfer meat to a plate. Reduce heat to medium and sauté finely chopped onion, carrot and celery for about 5 to 6 minutes, until soft. Sprinkle 2 tbs. flour over vegetables and cook for another 2 minutes. Return reserved marinade to Dutch oven and stir well. Return meat to Dutch oven and bring liquid to a boil over high heat. Cover, reduce heat to low and cook for about 2½ hours, until meat shows no resistance when pierced with the tip of a knife. Transfer meat to a platter and cover with foil to keep warm. Pour cooking liquid through a strainer into a saucepan and discard vegetables. Bring liquid to a boil over high heat and add tomato paste and crushed gingersnaps. Reduce heat to medium and cook, stirring frequently, for 5 to 6 minutes, until sauce is smooth and thickened. Taste sauce and add salt and pepper if needed. To serve, slice meat and coat with sauce.

BEEF, BEER AND ONION STEW (CARBONNADE À LA FLAMANDE)

Servings: 6

Bacon, onions and beer flavor this classic beef stew from Belgium. Serve with boiled or mashed potatoes and drink a Belgian Duvel or Trappist ale.

4 oz. thick-sliced bacon, cut into 1-inch pieces
3 lb. lean chuck or shoulder beef, cut into 1-inch cubes
4 large onions, about 2 lb., thinly sliced lengthwise from stem to root
2 cloves garlic, finely chopped

1 bottle (12 oz.) dark ale or porter
1 bay leaf
1 tsp. dried thyme
1 tbs. Dijon mustard
1 tbs. brown sugar
$\frac{1}{2}$ tsp. salt
freshly ground pepper to taste

Cook bacon pieces in a large skillet over medium heat until some fat is released and bacon is translucent, but not brown. Transfer bacon to a heavy 4- to 6-quart casserole or stockpot. Increase heat to high and brown beef cubes a few at a time in skillet until nicely browned on all sides. Place browned meat in casserole with bacon. Reduce heat to low and cook onions in skillet for 8 to 10 minutes, until onions are soft and lightly browned. Scrape up browned bits from the bottom of skillet. Add garlic and cook for 1 to 2 minutes. Add remaining ingredients, bring to a boil and pour over beef cubes. Simmer stew covered over low heat for 1 to $1\frac{1}{2}$ hours, until beef is tender.

GRILLED FLANK STEAK ADOBO

The chipotle chile in the marinade gives this steak a distinctive smoky character. Use canned chipotles in adobo sauce, which can be found in the Mexican food section of the supermarket or in specialty food stores. Serve with a crisp green salad and **Easy Baked Beans**, *page 63, or* **Potato Gratin**, *page 71. Drink an oatmeal stout or porter. To make sandwiches the next day, lightly warm meat in the microwave and place on some good bread that has been generously spread with mustard. Include some roasted red bell pepper strips for flavor and color.*

1 flank steak, about 1½ lb., well trimmed	2 tbs. vegetable oil
1 canned chipotle chile plus 1 tbs. adobo sauce	2 tbs. soy sauce
	juice of 1 lime
1 clove garlic, finely chopped	½ tsp. dried oregano

Place flank steak on a plate. Remove and discard stem and seeds from chile and chop finely. Place chile and 1 tbs. adobo sauce in a small bowl. Add garlic, oil, soy sauce, lime juice and oregano and mix well. Spoon mixture on both sides of steak and marinate at cool room temperature for 35 to 45 minutes. Grill on a hot grill or barbecue fire for about 6 minutes on the first side and 4 minutes on the second; beef should be pink in the middle. Transfer to a plate, cover loosely with foil and let rest for 10 minutes before carving. Holding knife at a 45-degree angle, slice thinly across the grain. Serve immediately.

GRILLED KOREAN BEEF
IN LETTUCE PACKAGES

Savory grilled beef pieces are rolled in a lettuce leaves with diced avocado and green onions. Ask your butcher to slice the meat very thinly. If you wish to slice the beef yourself, place it in the freezer for an hour before cutting. The partially frozen beef is much easier to slice than when it is at room temperature. This dish makes a great lunch, or serve it as an informal appetizer around the grill. Drink an Asian beer or India pale ale.

3 tbs. soy sauce
1 tbs. rice vinegar or dry sherry
1 tsp. toasted sesame oil
1/4 tsp. Tabasco Sauce
1 tbs. brown sugar
1 clove garlic, crushed
1 tsp. finely minced peeled ginger root
8-10 green onions, white part only
1 lb. thinly sliced beef sirloin or eye of round, about 1/8-inch thick,
   cut across the grain into 2-x-3-inch pieces
8-10 large iceberg lettuce leaves
1 avocado, cut into 1/2-inch cubes

Place soy sauce, rice vinegar, toasted sesame oil, Tabasco Sauce, brown sugar, garlic and ginger root in a blender container or food processor workbowl and process until smooth. Pour into a nonmetallic bowl. Slice 2 of the green onions thinly and add to bowl with sliced meat, stirring to coat meat with marinade. Cover and marinate at room temperature for 20 to 30 minutes. Cut remaining green onions into thin matchstick strips and place in a bowl of ice water until crisp. Drain onions and pat dry just before serving.

Heat grill to high. Drain meat and discard marinade. Grill for 1 to 2 minutes on each side, until just cooked through. Do not overcook.

To serve, place 1 to 2 slices hot grilled meat on a lettuce leaf and top with cubes of avocado and a few green onion strips. Fold over one end of lettuce leaf and roll up cigar fashion.

Britain's Bass Pale Ale bottles appear in Manet's painting of "Bar aux Folies-Bergere." 1881-82

CHILI

Chili and beer have a natural affinity. Mexican beer and a little chocolate give this version a Mexican slant. Traditionalists would not add beans, but would serve them alongside or with the chili spooned over them. Serve this in toasted bread bowls: eat the chili with a spoon; then, attack the delicious chili-soaked bread with a knife and fork. You can also serve the chili over rice or on its own.

1/4 lb. salt pork, cut into 3/8-inch cubes
2 lb. beef chuck, cut into 1/2-inch cubes
2 lb. pork shoulder, cut into 1/2-inch cubes
3 medium-sized yellow onions, diced
8 cloves garlic, finely chopped
1/2 cup chili powder
1/4 cup ground cumin
1 tbs. dried oregano
1 bottle (12 oz.) dark Mexican lager, such as Dos Equis
2 cans (14 1/2 oz. each) beef broth
1 can (14 1/2 oz.) ready-cut tomatoes
1 tsp. salt plus more to taste

freshly ground black pepper to taste
1 oz. unsweetened chocolate
juice of 1 lime
Tabasco Sauce or cayenne pepper to taste
1-2 tbs. cornmeal or masa harina, optional
3 cans (15 oz. each) black beans, drained
optional garnishes: sour cream, chopped fresh cilantro, lime slices, diced red onion, finely minced jalapeño chiles and shredded cheddar cheese
Bread Bowls, follow, optional

In a large heavy Dutch oven, cook salt pork over low heat until fat is released and cubes are lightly browned, but not crisp. With a slotted spoon, transfer salt pork to a plate. Increase heat to medium-high and cook beef and pork cubes a few at a time until browned on all sides; transfer browned meat to plate. Reduce heat to low and add onions. Cook onions slowly for 8 to 10 minutes, until soft and lightly browned. Scrape up browned bits on bottom of Dutch oven. Add garlic, chili powder, cumin and oregano and stir for 1 to 2 minutes. Return salt pork and meat cubes to Dutch oven. Add beer, beef broth, tomatoes, 1 tsp. salt and generous grinds of black pepper. Increase heat to high and bring to a boil. Stir in chocolate and lime juice. Reduce heat to low, cover and simmer gently for 1½ hours. Check meat for tenderness and cook longer if necessary. Taste for seasoning, adding salt, Tabasco or cayenne to taste. If you prefer a thicker chili, stir in cornmeal or masa harina and cook for 5 minutes. To serve, add black beans to chili and heat through. Serve in soup bowls or *Bread Bowls* on a plate and add desired garnishes.

BREAD BOWLS
6-8 round loaves bread, about 8 oz. each   olive oil

Heat oven to 300°. Cut off top ⅓ of each loaf and remove soft bread inside, leaving a ½-inch shell. Brush the inside of loaves with a small amount of olive oil and bake for 20 to 25 minutes, until lightly browned.

ITALIAN SAUSAGE CALZONES

Makes 6

These sausage- and mushroom-stuffed pies can be served hot or warm for lunch or supper. Drink your favorite pilsner or marzen. Make the filling and cool it while you are putting together the crust. The crust goes together quickly in a food processor and can be rolled out right away.

FILLING

2 Italian sausages, mild or hot,
  about ½ lb.
1 cup finely chopped onion
12 oz. white mushrooms, thinly sliced
salt and freshly ground pepper to taste

½ cup diced roasted red bell peppers
1 cup ricotta cheese
1½ cups coarsely shredded mozzarella
  cheese
1 egg, lightly beaten

CRUST

3 cups all-purpose flour
1½ tsp. baking powder
¾ tsp. salt

⅓ cup olive oil
⅓ cup amber ale or lager
1 egg

EGG WASH

1 egg yolk mixed with 1 tsp. water

For filling, remove sausages from casings and crumble into a heated medium skillet. Sauté sausage meat over medium-high heat until cooked through and lightly browned, using a spatula to break up larger pieces. Transfer sausage to a large plate and drain all but 1 tbs. fat from skillet. Add onion to skillet and sauté over medium heat for 2 to 3 minutes, until soft. Increase heat to high and add mushrooms. Season with salt and pepper and cook for 5 to 6 minutes until mushrooms are lightly browned and liquid is released. Transfer mushroom mixture to plate with sausage and spread out to cool. When barely warm, place sausage-mushroom mixture in a bowl, add remaining filling ingredients and mix well.

Heat oven to 375°. For crust, place flour, baking powder and salt in a food processor workbowl. Pulse 2 to 3 times to blend ingredients. Add olive oil, ale and egg and process for 1 minute, until ingredients are well mixed. Dough will have a grainy appearance and will not come together in a ball. Remove dough from bowl and place on a sheet of waxed paper. Press dough together into a log. Divide dough into 6 pieces, about 4 oz. each. Roll dough portions on a work surface into 6-inch circles.

Place 1/6 of the filling on half of each dough circle. Fold dough over filling and crimp edges tightly to seal. Brush top and sides of calzones with egg wash. Cut a 1-inch slit in the top of each calzone to let steam escape. Place calzones on a baking sheet and bake for 30 to 35 minutes, until nicely browned. Cool on a rack or serve immediately.

HUNGARIAN PORK GOULASH

Servings: 6

Make and serve this satisfying cold-weather dish with a dark lager or pale ale that is not too bitter. If you like, make this a day ahead up to the point of adding the sour cream. Reheat goulash while noodles cook and stir in sour cream just before serving.

2 lb. lean boneless pork loin
salt and pepper to taste
2 tbs. vegetable oil
1 tbs. butter
2 medium onions, thinly sliced
¾ cup dark lager or pale ale
2 cloves garlic, minced
2 tsp. hot Hungarian paprika
½ tsp. dill weed
2 tbs. tomato paste
1 can (14½ oz.) beef or chicken broth
⅔ cup sour cream
1 pkg. (8 oz.) egg noodles, cooked according to package directions
2 tbs. butter, melted
¼ cup chopped fresh parsley

Hops are thought to have been used to flavor and preserve beer in ancient Egypt, but fell out of favor. They were not commonly used again until the 16th century.

Cut pork loin across the grain into 1/4-inch-thick strips. Season with salt and pepper. Combine 1 tbs. of the oil and butter in a large heavy skillet over medium-high heat. When butter has melted, add 1/2 of the pork strips and brown lightly on both sides; set aside. Repeat process with remaining pork. Add remaining oil to skillet. Add onions and cook over low heat for 4 to 5 minutes to soften onions, scraping up brown bits on the bottom of skillet. Add 1/2 cup of the beer, cover and cook over low heat for about 20 minutes. Onions should be lightly browned and the beer evaporated. Add garlic, paprika, dill and tomato paste and return pork and any juices to skillet. Pour in broth and remaining beer. Bring to a simmer over medium heat, cover, reduce heat to low and simmer for about 30 minutes, until pork is tender. Remove cover, increase heat to medium and continue to cook for about 10 minutes, until liquid is slightly reduced. Remove pan from heat and stir in sour cream. Gently heat through over low heat, but do not boil. Taste and adjust seasonings. Toss hot cooked noodles with melted butter and parsley and arrange on heated plates. Spoon goulash over noodles.

SAUERKRAUT, POTATOES AND ASSORTED MEATS (CHOUCROUTE GARNIE)

This rich, hearty sauerkraut and sausage dish from Alsace, France, goes extremely well with beer. If you have access to a good deli, buy some freshly prepared sauerkraut. We like to cook the sausages separately so their texture is preserved and the sauerkraut remains lighter and less greasy. This is a great party dish to do ahead and reheat while the potatoes are cooking. Drink an Alsatian bitter. Pick 3 or 4 of each type of your favorite sausages.

2 cans (1 lb., 11 oz. each) sauerkraut, or about 3 lb. bulk sauerkraut
½ lb. thick-sliced bacon, cut into 1-inch pieces
1½ cups chopped onions
2 cloves garlic, finely chopped
1 tart green apple, cored, coarsely chopped
3 carrots, coarsely grated
1½ cups dry white wine
10 juniper berries, or ¼ cup gin

1 can (14½ oz.) chicken broth
1 bay leaf
1 tsp. dried thyme
8 small thin-cut smoked pork chops or 1 lb. sliced smoked pork loin
8-12 medium-sized red potatoes
9-12 cooked sausages, such as kielbasa, knackwurst and bratwurst
¼ cup finely chopped fresh parsley
2-3 prepared mustards, such as spicy brown, Dijon and whole grain

Taste sauerkraut. If it is very salty, soak in cold water in a bowl for 10 to 15 minutes; drain well. If it is not too salty, place in a strainer and rinse with cold water; drain well. In a large heavy stockpot or casserole, sauté bacon pieces over medium heat until translucent, but not brown. Remove bacon and set aside. Add onions to pot and sauté over medium heat for 6 to 8 minutes, until softened. Stir in garlic, apple and carrots and continue to cook for 1 to 2 minutes. Add drained sauerkraut to stockpot. Cook mixture over medium heat for 3 to 4 minutes. Add sautéed bacon, wine, juniper berries, chicken broth, bay leaf, thyme and a small amount of salt and pepper. Push pork chops down into sauerkraut. Cook covered over low heat for about 30 minutes. Add more liquid if needed. Taste and adjust seasonings.

While sauerkraut is cooking, boil potatoes in a separate pot until tender. Simmer sausages in 1 cup water for about 10 minutes, until heated through. Take care not to let sausage skins burst. Drain sausages on a plate.

To serve, heap sauerkraut in the center of a large platter. Arrange pork chops around sauerkraut. Cut each sausage into 3 or 4 pieces and arrange on platter around sauerkraut. Sprinkle potatoes with parsley and pass separately. Provide heated serving plates and pass mustards.

OVEN-ROASTED SPARERIBS

*These meaty brown spareribs are basted with a beer marinade. Bake some potatoes the last hour of roasting and serve with **Green Bean and Mushroom Salad**, page 47. Drink an amber or pale ale. If you like a sweeter, tomato-based barbecue sauce on your ribs, follow the recipe; then, brush ribs with your favorite purchased sauce and bake for another 5 to 10 minutes.*

3 lb. pork spareribs
1/4 cup cider vinegar
salt and freshly ground pepper
1 cup lager
1/3 cup brown sugar, packed
2 tsp. brown or Dijon mustard

2 tbs. soy sauce
1 tsp. hot Hungarian paprika
2 tbs. tomato paste
1 tbs. vegetable oil
salt and freshly ground pepper to taste

Heat oven to 375°. Line a baking pan with foil and spray a roasting rack with nonstick cooking spray and place in pan. Place ribs on rack, sprinkle with 2 tbs. of the cider vinegar and season with salt and pepper. Roast for 1 1/2 to 1 3/4 hours, until ribs are brown and meat pulls away from the bone.

While ribs are roasting, combine remaining 2 tbs. vinegar and other ingredients in a bowl. After 30 minutes of roasting, turn ribs over and baste with marinade. Turn and baste ribs every 15 minutes. Serve hot or reheat before serving.

PORK CHOPS WITH BEER-CAPER SAUCE

Boiled new potatoes or steamed rice and buttered carrots complement chops served in a creamy piquant sauce. Drink a marzen or India pale ale.

2 tbs. butter
6 pork loin chops, about 3/4-inch thick
1 tbs. flour
1 tbs. Dijon mustard
1/2 cup beef broth

1/2 cup pale ale
salt and freshly ground pepper to taste
2/3 cup sour cream
2 tsp. capers, rinsed, drained
1/4 cup finely chopped fresh parsley

Heat butter in a large heavy skillet over medium-high heat and brown pork chops for about 2 minutes on each side. Remove chops from skillet. Stir flour and mustard into pan drippings and cook for 1 minute. Gradually stir in beef broth, ale, salt and pepper until mixture is smooth and comes to a boil. Return chops to skillet. Reduce heat to low, cover and simmer for 10 to 12 minutes, until chops are cooked through and tender. Stir in sour cream and capers and heat gently, but do not boil. Taste and adjust seasonings. Sprinkle with parsley and serve immediately.

PORK CHOPS STUFFED WITH APPLES AND DRIED CHERRIES

Savory fruit-stuffed pork chops are baked in porter. Ask your butcher to cut pockets in the chops. Use Golden Delicious or Granny Smith apples for the stuffing, which can be made a day ahead if you like. Serve this with creamy polenta or mashed potatoes. Drink an amber or apricot ale.

2 tbs. butter
1 medium onion, finely chopped
2 tart cooking apples, peeled, cored, diced
½ cup dried tart cherries or cranberries
2 tbs. golden raisins
2 tbs. balsamic vinegar
salt and freshly ground pepper to taste
1 cup plus 2 tbs. porter or amber ale
6 large pork loin chops, about 1-inch thick,
   with a 3-inch pocket
1 tbs. olive oil
1 cup chicken broth
1 tbs. cornstarch dissolved in 2 tbs. cold water

Ice-making machines and ice-cooled rooms were invented in the 1860s, which allowed brewers to produce lager year-round.

Melt butter in a large skillet. Sauté onion and apples over low heat for 10 minutes. Add cherries, raisins, vinegar, salt, pepper and 2 tbs. beer and cook for 2 to 3 minutes. Cool slightly.

Heat oven to 325°. Season inside of pork chop pockets with salt and pepper and stuff with apple-cherry mixture. Heat oil in a large skillet over high heat. Brown pork chops in batches on both sides, about 2 to 3 minutes per side. Place chops in a covered baking dish. Pour 1 cup beer and chicken broth in skillet and bring to a boil, scraping up any browned bits. Pour mixture over chops, cover and bake for 40 to 45 minutes, until chops are cooked through and tender. Transfer chops to a plate and stir dissolved cornstarch into liquid. Bring to a boil over high heat on the stovetop and cook for 1 to 2 minutes until sauce thickens. Check seasonings, adding more salt and pepper if needed. Serve on heated plates and spoon sauce over chops.

TOMATO PORK CURRY

The quick curry sauce in this recipe can be made in the time it takes the rice to cook. Serve with an Irish lager or India pale ale.

1 pork tenderloin, about ¾ lb., well trimmed
2 tbs. soy sauce
1 tbs. cornstarch
1 tbs. lemon juice
pinch white pepper
8 plum tomatoes
3 tbs. vegetable oil
1 cup chopped onion
1 tbs. curry powder
1 cup chicken broth
2 tsp. brown sugar
1 tbs. cornstarch dissolved in 2 tbs. cold water
Tabasco Sauce to taste
hot steamed rice
condiments: chutney, chopped peanuts,
    toasted coconut, optional

William Painter patented the crown bottle cap in 1892. Within a few years, corks and less effective closures for beer bottles were replaced with Painter's cap. The cap remains virtually unchanged today, except for a slight modification, which allows it to be twisted off. Painter founded the Crown Cork and Seal Company, which is still a major producer of crown bottle caps.

Cut pork tenderloin into ⅛-inch slices and place in a small bowl with soy sauce, cornstarch, lemon juice and white pepper. Toss to coat meat evenly. Remove stem ends of tomatoes and cut into quarters lengthwise. Scoop out seeds with your fingers and discard. Cut each wedge in half crosswise.

Heat 2 tbs. of the oil over high heat in a medium skillet and sauté pork until it loses its pink color and turns gray. Transfer pork to a plate, reduce heat to medium and add remaining oil and onion to pan. Sauté onion over medium-low heat for 4 to 5 minutes, until onion softens, but is not brown. Scrape up brown bits from the bottom of pan. Add curry powder and cook for about 1 minute, until aroma is released. Add chicken broth and sugar. Return pork to pan and add tomato pieces. When mixture is simmering, cover and cook for 3 to 4 minutes. Add ½ of the dissolved cornstarch to skillet. Cook for 1 minute to thicken sauce. If sauce is too thin, add more cornstarch mixture. Add Tabasco to taste. Serve immediately with hot rice. Pass small bowls of condiments if desired.

ROASTED PORK WITH BROWN ALE SAUCE

Serve this as the main course for a company dinner with oven-roasted potatoes and carrots. If you have leftover roast, make sandwiches on rye bread with spicy brown mustard and dill pickle slices. Drink a golden or brown ale.

3 lb. boneless pork loin, fat trimmed to
   a thin layer
salt and freshly ground pepper
2 tbs. soy sauce
1 clove garlic, finely chopped
1 quarter-sized piece ginger root,
   peeled, finely chopped

1 tbs. brown sugar
1/2 cup water
1 cup brown ale or honey porter
1 cup chicken broth
12-16 dried prunes
1 tbs. cornstarch dissolved in 2 tbs. cold
   water

Heat oven to 350°. Rub pork roast with salt and pepper. Combine soy sauce, garlic, ginger and brown sugar in a small bowl and spoon over pork. Place pork in a roasting pan with water. Roast for about 1 1/2 hours, until pork reaches an internal temperature of about 165°. Transfer pork to a platter and cover with foil. Pour ale and chicken broth into pan, bring to a boil on the stovetop and scrape up brown bits from the bottom of pan. Remove from heat. Strain pan juices into a small saucepan and skim and discard fat. Add dried prunes and simmer over medium heat for 5 to 10 minutes. Stir in dissolved cornstarch and cook for 2 to 3 minutes, until thickened. Adjust seasonings. To serve, slice pork and spoon sauce and prunes over individual servings.

HAM WITH APRICOT-ALE SAUCE

Servings: 4

Ham pairs deliciously with a dried apricot-ale sauce. Serve with **Potato Gratin**, *page 71, and fresh steamed asparagus.*

2 tbs. butter
2 tbs. minced shallots
1/3 cup finely chopped dried apricots
1 tbs. lemon juice
2 tsp. brown sugar
1/2 cup chicken broth
1/2 cup apricot or pale ale

pinch mace or powdered ginger
pinch cayenne pepper
2 tsp. cornstarch dissolved in 1 tbs. cold water
1 ham steak, about 1 lb., or other cooked ham, heated

Melt butter in a small saucepan. Add shallot and sauté over medium heat for 1 to 2 minutes, until softened. Add remaining ingredients, except cornstarch and ham, and bring to a boil over high heat. Reduce heat to low and simmer for 5 minutes. Add a small amount of the cornstarch mixture and continue to cook until sauce thickens to the consistency of heavy cream. Add more cornstarch mixture if needed. Slice ham into serving pieces. Spoon sauce over ham.

VARIATION: HAM WITH CHERRY-WHEAT ALE SAUCE
Substitute cherry wheat ale for apricot ale and dried cherries for dried apricots.

JAMAICAN-STYLE CURRIED LAMB

Servings: 6

*Drink a Samuel Smith's pale ale or a Jamaican Red Stripe lager with this spicy curry. Serve with lots of steamed rice and **Avocado Citrus Salad**, page 44. Ask the butcher to slice the leg of lamb into 1-inch pieces through the bone.*

4 lb. shank-end leg of lamb, cut into 1-
    inch pieces, or 3 lb. lamb stew meat
1 tbs. vegetable oil
2 large onions, chopped
3 cloves garlic, finely chopped
2 tsp. finely chopped ginger root
1 habanero chile, or 4 jalapeño chiles,
    seeded, finely chopped
3 tbs. curry powder
1 can (14½ oz.) ready-cut tomatoes

1 can (14½ oz.) chicken broth
water
1 bay leaf
1 tsp. salt
generous amount freshly ground pepper
1 tbs. red wine vinegar
1 tbs. butter, optional
1 tbs. flour, optional
2 tbs. chopped fresh cilantro

Trim excess fat from lamb. Heat vegetable oil in a large heavy 5- to 6-quart stockpot or Dutch oven. Over high heat, brown lamb cubes on all sides, a few at a time. Transfer browned pieces to a platter. Reduce heat to low, add onions and stir to scrape up brown bits on the bottom of pan. Sauté onions for about 8 to 10 minutes, until soft and golden, about 8 to 10 minutes. Add garlic, ginger, chile and curry powder and cook for 1 to 2 minutes to release flavors. Return meat to pan and add tomatoes, chicken broth and enough water to barely cover meat. Add bay leaf, salt and pepper. Bring to a boil over high heat. Reduce heat to low and gently simmer uncovered for 1 hour. Test meat for doneness; it should be very tender. Skim fat from the surface of stew and discard. Add vinegar and cook for another minute.

If you desire a thicker sauce, melt butter in a small saucepan, add flour and cook for 1 to 2 minutes. Spoon in about 1 cup cooking liquid from stew and cook, stirring, until mixture starts to thicken. Add mixture to pot with lamb and cook for 3 to 4 minutes, until stew thickens.

To serve, pour stew into a serving dish and sprinkle with cilantro.

CHARCOAL-GRILLED LEG OF LAMB

Servings: 8-10

*A marinated, butterflied leg of lamb makes a great dinner party entrée. Ask your butcher to bone and butterfly the lamb. Serve with **Almond and Dried Cherry Pilaf**, page 69. Drink a brown ale or honey porter.*

5-6 lb. leg of lamb, boned, butterflied,
    well trimmed
salt and freshly ground pepper
¼ cup olive oil
3 tbs. lemon juice
½ cup porter or stout
½ cup finely chopped onion

2 cloves garlic, finely chopped
1 tbs. spicy brown or Dijon mustard
2 tsp. brown sugar
1 tsp. dried marjoram
dash red pepper flakes, or 1 jalapeño
    chile, seeded, minced

With a sharp knife, make a few cuts through the thickest part of lamb so that it lies as flat as possible and has a uniform thickness. Rub lamb on both sides with salt and pepper and place in a nonreactive 9-x-13-inch pan. Combine remaining ingredients in a small bowl, mix well, and pour over lamb, coating both sides. Cover tightly and refrigerate for at least 4 hours or overnight. Turn lamb once or twice while it is marinating. Remove lamb from refrigerator 1½ hours before grilling. Prepare a hot barbecue fire or heat grill to high. Drain liquid from lamb and grill for about 12 to 15 minutes on each side for medium rare. Cut into thin slices to serve.

BEER WITH SEAFOOD DISHES

PAIRING SEAFOOD DISHES WITH BEER

Fish pairs well with many of the wheat beers. Hefe-weizen or German and Bavarian "white beers" work well for both for cooking and drinking. Pale ales and Belgium's Duvel ale are also very complementary to seafood. Fresh-cooked crab and grilled fish go as well with beer as as they do with wine.

Classic uses of beer with seafood include poaching salmon, and steaming shrimp or clams. Beer-based batters are particularly popular for frying fish and shrimp. Use beers that are light in color and style for seafood sauces and marinades.

Try *Sea Bass with Lemon Caper Sauce* and *Red Snapper Provençal with beer*. Beer is also the preferred beverage with *Clam and Garlic Pizza*, *Szechuan Hot Garlic Shrimp* and *Fish Tacos with Spicy Cabbage Slaw*.

Chicago had several operating breweries, including the very large Chicago Brewing Company, at the time of the great fire in 1871. Wisconsin breweries, especially those in Milwaukee, were quick to supply the beer needs of Chicago while it was rebuilding. The Chicago Brewing Company never reopened and Chicago hasn't had an important regional brewery since the fire.

BEER-BATTERED FRIED SHRIMP OR FISH

*This easy beer batter is also great for vegetables. Make the batter at least 2 hours ahead. Use a good thermometer to make sure the frying oil is at the proper temperature. Don't fry too many pieces at one time and let the oil return to temperature before frying the next batch. Serve with **Red Cabbage and Fennel Slaw**, page 47, or **Caesar Salad**, page 48.*

1 cup all-purpose flour
2/3 cup plus 2 tbs. lager or pale ale
1/2 tsp. salt
1 tsp. baking powder
pinch cayenne pepper

1/4 tsp. paprika
4 cups peanut or corn oil
1 lb. shrimp, peeled, deveined, butterflied, or 1 lb. fish fillets cut into 1-x-3-inch "fingers"

Whisk together 2/3 cup of the flour, 2/3 cup beer, salt, baking powder, cayenne and paprika in a small bowl and let stand at room temperature for at least 2 hours. Just before using, whisk in remaining 2 tbs. beer and pour batter into a shallow dish or pie plate. Place remaining 1/3 cup flour in another shallow dish. Pour oil into a heavy deep-sided pan and heat until a deep-fat thermometer registers 375°. Lightly dust shrimp or fish with flour, coat with batter and let excess drip off for a few seconds. Fry a few pieces at a time in hot oil until golden brown. Drain on paper towels. Serve hot.

BEER-POACHED SALMON STEAKS WITH CAPER SAUCE

*Beer makes a flavorful poaching liquid for individual fish steaks or a larger piece of fish. Serve the cooked fish hot or cold with **Caper Sauce**, which can be made ahead and refrigerated.*

1 bottle (12 oz.) hefe-weizen or
    wheat beer
1 lemon, thinly sliced
2-3 green onions, coarsely chopped
1 quarter-sized piece ginger root,
    unpeeled
1 sprig fresh thyme

1 bay leaf
3-4 whole peppercorns
1/4 tsp. salt
4 salmon steaks, about 1-inch thick
finely chopped fresh parsley for garnish
Caper Sauce, follows

In a skillet large enough to hold fish pieces in a single layer, combine beer, lemon, green onions, ginger, thyme, bay leaf, peppercorns and salt. Bring liquid to a boil over high heat. Reduce heat to low and simmer for 10 minutes. Slide fish into liquid, cover and simmer over low heat for 8 to 10 minutes, until salmon has turned opaque and is slightly springy when pressed. Line a platter with paper towels; remove cooked fish from liquid and place on paper towels to drain. Blot liquid from top of fish. Place salmon steaks on individual serving plates, sprinkle with parsley and serve hot, warm or cold with *Caper Sauce*.

CAPER SAUCE

½ cup mayonnaise
½ cup sour cream
1 tbs. Dijon mustard
2 tsp. lemon juice

3 tbs. capers, drained, coarsely chopped
generous amount ground white pepper
2 tsp. finely chopped fresh chives

Combine ingredients in a small bowl and mix well. Chill until ready to serve.

NOTE: If poaching a whole fish or large chunk of fish, double the amount of liquid in the recipe and use a deep pan that is just large enough to accommodate fish. Liquid should come halfway up the sides of fish. Wrap fish in cheesecloth, tying the ends with kitchen string to leave "handles." Turn fish over halfway through poaching.

Lagers generally can be served with dishes where one would drink a white wine; ales can generally be served in place of red wine.

CHINESE-STYLE SWEET AND SOUR FISH

Servings: 4

Serve this dish with hot steamed rice to catch the delicious sauce. Rock cod, sea bass, swordfish or other firm-fleshed fish works well. Drink with a Tsing Tao or another Asian beer.

1-1½ lb. firm fleshed skinless fish fillets
salt and pepper
flour for dusting
¼ cup vegetable oil
1 bunch green onions, white part only, cut into matchstick strips
2 jalapeño chiles, seeded, cut into matchstick strips
2 quarter-sized pieces ginger root, peeled, finely minced
1 clove garlic, finely chopped

½ cup chicken broth
1 tbs. soy sauce
1 tbs. dry sherry or Shao Xing rice wine
½ tsp. Tabasco Jalapeño Sauce
2 tsp. cider vinegar
2 tsp. brown sugar
1 tsp. toasted sesame oil
1 tbs. cornstarch dissolved in 2 tbs. cold water
hot steamed rice

Cut fish fillets into 1-inch cubes, sprinkle with salt and pepper and lightly dust with flour. Heat a large skillet that will hold fish in a single layer over medium heat and add vegetable oil when hot. Gently stir-fry fish for about 5 minutes, until lightly browned. Transfer fish to a platter. Discard all but 1 tbs. oil from skillet. Add onions, chiles, ginger and garlic and sauté for 1 minute. Add chicken broth, soy sauce, sherry, Tabasco, vinegar, brown sugar and toasted sesame oil and bring to a boil. Return fish to pan and simmer for 1 to 2 minutes. Pour in about half of the dissolved cornstarch mixture and stir until thickened. Sauce should be the consistency of heavy cream. Add a little more dissolved cornstarch if necessary. Serve on heated plates with steamed rice.

During the Middle Ages, beer was widely consumed. Since beer was boiled during production, it was a safer drink than water, which was often contaminated. The alcohol and hops in the beer also offered some protection from bacterial growth.

CLAM AND GARLIC PIZZA

Servings: 4

Make sure everyone in the crowd has a piece of this garlicky pizza. The delicious, crisp crust goes together quickly with a food processor. Bread flour will make a chewier crust, but all-purpose flour also works well. Baking on a pizza stone will give a nice crisp crust. Drink a pale ale or your favorite lager.

EASY PIZZA CRUST

1 cup pale ale
1 pkg. fast-acting yeast
2½ cups bread or all-purpose flour

1 tsp. salt
2 tbs. olive oil

TOPPING

⅔ cup prepared pizza sauce
1 can (10 oz.) baby clams, drained,
   coarsely chopped, or 2 cans
   (6½ oz. each) chopped clams
large dash red pepper flakes

8-10 cloves garlic, thinly sliced
2 cups shredded mozzarella cheese
1 small red onion, thinly sliced
¼ cup finely chopped fresh parsley
salt and freshly ground pepper to taste

For crust, pour beer into a saucepan and heat until just warm to the touch. Place warm beer in a food processor workbowl, sprinkle with yeast and pulse until dissolved. Add 1 cup of the flour and pulse. Let rest for 15 minutes; the mixture should be bubbly. Add remaining flour, salt and olive oil and process for about 1 minute, until dough forms a ball. Dough will be quite soft. Remove dough from workbowl and place in a lightly oiled bowl. Cover and let rise until doubled in size, about 45 minutes.

Heat oven to 450°, with pizza stone if desired. Pat, stretch or roll dough into a 13-inch circle on a piece of parchment or foil. Let rest for a few minutes before adding topping.

Spread crust with pizza sauce. Distribute a layer each of clams, red pepper flakes, garlic, cheese and onion slices over pizza sauce and season with salt and pepper. Transfer pizza to pizza stone or a large baking sheet. If using pizza stone, bake for about 12 to 14 minutes, until brown and bubbly. If using baking sheet, place on the lowest oven rack and bake for 15 to 18 minutes, until brown and bubbly. Sprinkle with parsley just before serving.

GRILLED SHRIMP AND MANGO SALAD

Servings: 3-4

These shrimp are also delicious as an appetizer; grill some when you have the grill started for another main course. You can substitute ripe peach or apricot slices in season for the mango. Drink a hefe-weisen or golden pilsner.

MARINADE

1 tbs. vegetable oil
2 tsp. finely chopped onion or shallot
1 tbs. lemon juice
1 tbs. ketchup

$\frac{1}{2}$ cup apricot or amber ale
1 tsp. prepared horseradish
1 tbs. soy sauce

1 lb. medium shrimp, about 30

DRESSING

2 tbs. full-flavored olive oil
1 tbs. sherry vinegar

2 tsp. finely minced shallot
salt and freshly ground pepper to taste

SALAD

5-6 cups mixed salad greens
1 small ripe avocado, thinly sliced

1 small ripe mango or papaya, peeled,
  sliced or diced

For marinade, combine ingredients in a small saucepan. Bring to a boil over high heat. Reduce heat to low and simmer for 3 to 4 minutes. Remove from heat and cool to room temperature.

Peel and devein shrimp. Pour cooled marinade over shrimp and let stand for 15 to 20 minutes. Heat grill to medium hot. Thread shrimp on metal or presoaked wooden skewers. Grill for about 3 minutes on each side, until shrimp turn pink and are slightly firm to the touch. Take care not to overcook.

For dressing, whisk together olive oil, vinegar, shallot, salt and pepper in a large bowl. Add salad greens and toss to coat greens with dressing. Arrange salad greens on a serving platter or individual plates. Scatter avocado and mango slices evenly over greens. Arrange shrimp over salad and serve immediately.

Czech Pilsner Urquell lager was first introduced in 1842. The beer was an instant hit and became a model that brewers the world over tried to duplicate. Pilsner Urquell was first imported into the United States in 1856.

SZECHUAN HOT GARLIC SHRIMP

Servings: 3-4

A pilsner or Chinese beer goes well with this spicy shrimp dish. Serve with hot cooked rice, and broccoli or asparagus cooked tender-crisp. The optional step of marinating the shrimp with salt firms and freshens them, and should be done just before cooking.

1 lb. medium shrimp, peeled, deveined
¼ cup kosher or sea salt, optional
1 large red or green bell pepper
1 large white onion
1 tsp. sugar
2 tbs. soy sauce
1 tbs. Shao Xing rice wine
2 tsp. white vinegar
2 tbs. clam juice or chicken broth
1 tsp. hot chile oil, optional

3 tbs. peanut or canola oil
3 large cloves garlic, minced
2 tsp. minced ginger root
2 jalapeño chiles, seeded, finely
    chopped
2 tsp. cornstarch dissolved in 1 tbs. cold
    water
1 tsp. toasted sesame oil
hot steamed rice

If desired, place shrimp in a small bowl with 2 tbs. of the Kosher salt. Toss to mix well and let stand for 10 minutes. Rinse well. Toss with remaining 2 tbs. Kosher salt. Let stand for 5 minutes. Rinse well and drain on paper towels.

Stem and seed red pepper and cut into 1-x-1½-inch rectangles. Peel onion, cut in half from stem to root, separate sections and cut into pieces the same size as pepper. Combine sugar, soy sauce, rice wine, white vinegar, clam juice and hot chile oil, if using, in a small bowl and mix well.

Heat peanut oil over high heat in a wok or large frying pan. When almost smoking, add garlic, ginger and jalapeño. Stir-fry for a few seconds, but do not allow to burn. Add shrimp and stir-fry for 20 seconds. Add pepper and onion pieces and stir-fry for 20 seconds. Add soy sauce mixture to vegetables and stir until well combined. Pour in cornstarch mixture, reduce heat to medium-low and cook for another 1 to 2 minutes, until sauce thickens. Sprinkle with toasted sesame oil and serve immediately in a warm serving bowl or on warm plates with steamed rice.

Foods with a lot of spice, vinegar, salt or chiles all go better with beer than with wine.

THAI SHRIMP CURRY

Serve this spicy, creamy curry over hot steamed rice and drink a pilsner or Thai beer, such as Singha. If you like, sprinkle the dish with chopped peanuts.

1 cup hefe-weizen or wheat beer
3 jalapeño chiles, seeded, finely
    chopped
4 cloves garlic, finely chopped
2 tsp. grated peeled ginger root
1 tbs. paprika
½ tsp. turmeric
1 tbs. ground coriander
½ tsp. ground cumin
1 tbs. sugar

1 can (14 oz.) unsweetened coconut milk
grated peel (zest) and juice of 1 lime
salt and freshly ground pepper to taste
2 tsp. cornstarch mixed with 1 tbs. cold
    water
1 lb. large shrimp, peeled and deveined
coarsely chopped fresh cilantro leaves
    for garnish
hot steamed rice

Combine beer, chiles, garlic, ginger, paprika, turmeric, coriander, cumin and sugar in a medium saucepan. Bring to a boil over high heat. Reduce heat to low and simmer for 15 minutes. Add coconut milk, lime peel, lime juice, salt and pepper and return to a boil. Stir in cornstarch mixture and cook for 2 to 3 minutes, until sauce thickens. Add shrimp and cook for about 3 minutes, until shrimp turn pink. Adjust seasonings. Sprinkle with cilantro leaves and serve over hot rice.

SICILIAN-STYLE GRILLED FISH

Servings: 4

A garlic and oregano marinade spices up halibut, sea bass, snapper or other firm-fleshed fish. Serve with a wheat beer or pale ale, a crisp salad and baked potatoes.

1/2 cup olive oil
3 tbs. lemon juice
2 cloves garlic, finely minced
1 1/2 tsp. dried oregano
3 tbs. finely chopped fresh parsley
salt and freshly ground pepper
   to taste
4 fish fillets, about 6 oz. each

The color of a beer does not always indicate body or alcoholic strength. In other words, a darker beer, such as a porter, is not necessarily higher in alcohol and heavier in body than a lighter beer, such as a pilsner.

Combine olive oil, lemon juice, garlic, oregano, parsley, salt and pepper in a small bowl and whisk until well combined. Place fish fillets on a plate or in a nonmetallic pan and coat with marinade. Marinate for 20 minutes.

Heat grill to medium. Remove fish from marinade and grill for 3 to 4 minutes on each side.

RED SNAPPER PROVENÇAL

Servings: 4

Pair this fish in garlicky tomato sauce with steamed rice and a golden lager or pilsner.

1/4 cup full-flavored olive oil
1/2 cup chopped onion
1/2 cup finely chopped fresh fennel,
   including some feathery tops
3 cloves garlic, finely chopped
4 plum tomatoes, seeded, chopped
1/3 cup amber or pale ale
grated peel (zest) and juice of 1 orange
1 tbs. tomato paste

1/4 cup coarsely chopped kalamata or
   other brine-cured black olives
1 tbs. drained capers
1/4 tsp. dried tarragon
4 red snapper fillets or other firm fish
   fillets, about 6 oz. each
salt and freshly ground pepper to taste
flour for dredging

Heat 2 tbs. of the olive oil in a heavy saucepan or skillet. Sauté onion and fennel over medium-low heat for 10 to 12 minutes. Add garlic, tomatoes, beer, orange juice and tomato paste and cook over medium-high heat for about 8 to 10 minutes, until juice from tomatoes is released and sauce thickens slightly. Remove from heat and add olives, capers, tarragon, orange peel, salt and pepper; keep warm.

Lightly dust fish with salt, pepper and flour. Heat remaining 2 tbs. olive oil over medium-high heat in a large skillet. Sauté fish for about 3 to 4 minutes on each side, until nicely browned. Serve immediately on warm plates and spoon sauce over fish.

SEA BASS WITH LEMON-CAPER SAUCE

Servings: 4

Firm-fleshed sea bass, halibut or swordfish steaks are easily cooked to moist perfection using this simple method. Serve with a wheat beer or your favorite ale.

4 sea bass or other fish steaks, about
    8 oz. each, 1-1½ inches thick
salt and freshly ground pepper
flour for dusting
1 tbs. vegetable oil
¼ cup chicken broth
¼ cup light-bodied lager or ale

1 tbs. butter
1 tbs. lemon juice
1 tbs. stone-ground mustard
2 tbs. drained capers
1 tsp. cornstarch dissolved in 2 tsp. cold
    water or beer
salt and freshly ground pepper to taste

Heat oven to 425°. Pat fish dry with paper towels, season both sides with salt and pepper and lightly dust with flour. Heat oil over medium heat in an ovenproof skillet large enough to hold fish steaks in a single layer. Just before oil starts to smoke, add fish and sauté for 2 minutes. Turn fish over and cook for 1 minute. Place skillet in oven and bake until fish flakes easily, about 7 minutes.

While fish bakes, bring chicken broth and beer to a boil in a small saucepan and cook until reduced to ⅓ cup. Stir in butter, lemon juice, mustard and capers. Add cornstarch mixture, bring to a boil and cook until sauce thickens. Season with salt and pepper. Remove fish from skillet, blot dry with paper towels and serve on heated plates with sauce.

FISH TACOS WITH SPICY CABBAGE SLAW

Makes 10

Crisp taco shells offer a nice texture contrast to the fish. Hefe-weisen or pilsner pairs perfectly. Allow each person to assemble his or her own taco by spooning some of the cabbage slaw into a taco shell, adding a few fish chunks and topping with a few cilantro leaves. Pass your favorite hot sauce for those who like their food really spicy.

2 cups finely shredded green
    cabbage
1/2 cup coarsely grated carrot
1/2 cup matchstick-sized strips red bell
    pepper
4 green onions, white part only, finely
    chopped
1 small jalapeño chile, seeded, finely
    minced
1 cup finely chopped pineapple, mango
    or orange pieces
2 tbs. mayonnaise

2 tbs. sour cream
2 tbs. lemon juice
1/2 tsp. prepared horseradish
salt and freshly ground pepper to taste
10 preformed regular-sized taco shells
2 tbs. vegetable oil
1 lb. thin fish fillets, such as sole,
    orange roughy or flounder
salt and pepper
flour for dusting
fresh cilantro leaves for garnish

Combine cabbage, carrot, red pepper, onions, jalapeño and pineapple in a salad bowl. Mix together mayonnaise, sour cream, lemon juice, horseradish, salt and pepper in a small bowl. Pour dressing over vegetable mixture and toss to coat vegetables.

Warm taco shells in a hot oven according to package directions.

Season fillets with salt and pepper and lightly dust with flour. Heat oil in a nonstick skillet over medium heat until quite hot. Sauté fish for about 3 minutes on each side. Fish should be cooked through, but still moist. Remove fish and cut into ½-inch pieces. Serve in warm taco shells with cabbage slaw and garnish with cilantro leaves.

In warm weather, just before pouring beer, swirl an ice cube or two in a heavy glass to cool it to about the temperature of the chilled beer. Dump out the ice and shake the water out of the glass. Pour beer immediately.

BEER WITH DESSERTS

PAIRING DESSERTS WITH BEER

With the wide range of beer styles available, it is no surprise that many can be placed in the dessert category, both for cooking and drinking. Oatmeal and triple stouts, Belgium lambics, some fruit-flavored beers, Scotch and Trappist ales and a few special holiday beers are richer and somewhat sweeter than traditional brews.

Raspberry-flavored beer teams with chocolate to make a terrific *Chocolate Raspberry Beer Cake*. Porters and stouts complement cinnamon, ginger and nutmeg, such as in the *Stout Gingerbread* and *Pecan-Porter Spice Cake*. Triple bock is reminiscent of a rich madeira or cream sherry. It holds its own when drunk with fragrant spice cakes or cookies, and is used here in *Triple Bock Baked Apples*. The intense raspberry flavors in Belgian framboise lambic inspired the *Raspberry Lambic Ice Cream Floats* and *Peach Melba with Raspberry Lambic*.

For drinking, the same beers used in dessert recipes work well as accompaniments. For example, raspberry lambic's fruit essence and light effervescence make it a refreshing partner for ripe summer-sweet strawberries, peaches or raspberries. While triple bock and lambics are fairly expensive, one bottle will serve 3 to 4 people for dessert. Give a dessert party and experiment with some dessert and beer combinations.

CHOCOLATE-RASPBERRY BEER CAKE

Servings: 10

Weizenberry, raspberry-flavored wheat beer, provides some of the liquid for this moist chocolate cake. The hint of raspberry in the cake is amplified with the raspberry frosting. You can also use your favorite chocolate frosting. Substitute a Belgian raspberry lambic or other fruit-flavored beer if you like. This is a terrific cake for a buffet or to take to a potluck. To melt chocolate, place chopped chocolate in a microwavable dish. Heat on MEDIUM for 4 to 5 minutes, checking frequently. Or, melt chocolate in a bowl over a small pan of simmering water.

2¼ cups sifted cake flour
2 tsp. baking soda
½ tsp. salt
½ cup butter
2½ cups brown sugar, packed
3 eggs
3 oz. unsweetened chocolate, chopped, melted
½ cup buttermilk
1 cup weizenberry ale, heated to just to boiling
2 tsp. vanilla extract
Raspberry Icing, follows

As you would with wine, serve lighter, simpler beers early in the meal and progress to darker, heavier styles throughout the feast.

Heat oven to 375°. Butter a 9-x-13-inch pan and lightly dust pan with flour. Sift together cake flour, soda and salt and set aside. With an electric mixer, cream butter and sugar together until fluffy. Add eggs one at a time and mix until well combined. Stir in melted chocolate. Add a small amount of sifted flour mixture to bowl and stir well. Continue to add flour alternately with buttermilk, stirring until smooth. When mixture is well mixed and smooth, stir in hot beer and vanilla extract. Batter will be quite thin. Pour into prepared baking pan and bake for 35 to 40 minutes, until top is firm to the touch and a toothpick inserted in the center of cake comes out clean. Remove pan from oven and place on a cooling rack. When cool, frost with *Raspberry Icing*.

RASPBERRY ICING

3 tbs. butter, softened
2 tbs. seedless raspberry preserves
2 cups sifted confectioners' sugar

1 tsp. vanilla extract
2-4 tbs. heavy cream

In a small bowl, cream together butter and raspberry preserves. Gradually stir in confectioners' sugar, mixing until very smooth. Add vanilla extract and 2 tbs. cream, beating well. If icing seems too stiff to spread easily, mix in 1 to 2 tbs. cream. Spread icing over top of cooled cake.

PECAN-PORTER SPICE CAKE

Serve this not-too-sweet cake for coffee, brunch or with a scoop of ice cream for dessert. It is also wonderful when made with cream ale or stout.

½ cup porter
¼ cup vegetable oil
½ cup molasses
1 cup brown sugar, packed
½ tsp. finely grated ginger root
2 eggs, lightly beaten
1½ cups all-purpose flour

½ tsp. baking soda
½ tsp. baking powder
1 tsp. cinnamon
¼ tsp. nutmeg
¼ tsp. salt
1 cup chopped toasted pecans

Heat oven to 350°. Oil and lightly flour an 8-inch square baking pan. Pour porter in a small saucepan and bring just to a boil. Remove from heat and pour into a bowl. Add oil, molasses, brown sugar and ginger and stir with a large wooden spoon until well blended. Add beaten eggs and stir to combine. Mix in remaining ingredients, except for pecans, until batter is smooth. Stir in nuts and pour into prepared baking pan. Bake for 35 to 40 minutes, until top is firm to the touch and a toothpick inserted in the center of cake comes out clean. Remove from oven and cool on a rack. Cut into squares to serve.

STOUT GINGERBREAD

*A full-bodied stout emphasizes the molasses and spice flavors in this old-fashioned gingerbread. Serve with a dollop of whipped cream or some **Honey Raspberry Ale-Poached Apples**, page 156.*

1 bottle (12 oz.) stout or dark ale	2 tsp. baking soda
6 tbs. butter, room temperature	1½ tsp. ground ginger
½ cup sugar	1 tsp. ground allspice
¾ cup molasses	1 tsp. cinnamon
2 eggs	¼ tsp. ground cloves
2¼ cups all-purpose flour	¼ tsp. salt

Heat oven to 350°. Butter an 8-inch square baking pan and lightly dust with flour. Pour stout into a small saucepan and bring to a boil. Cook over high heat for 3 to 4 minutes, until reduced to 1¼ cups. Remove from heat. With an electric mixer, cream together butter and sugar until light and fluffy. Add molasses and eggs and mix until well combined. Sift flour, soda, spices and salt together. Alternately add small amounts of flour mixture and warm stout to butter mixture, mixing well after each addition. Spoon batter into prepared baking pan. Bake for 45 to 50 minutes, until top is firm and a toothpick inserted in the center comes out clean. Cool on a rack and cut into squares to serve.

HONEY RASPBERRY ALE-POACHED APPLES

Servings: 4-6

Try poaching apples in fruit-flavored beer or lambic. Maple porter also works well. If you like, top apples with a little heavy cream or a scoop of vanilla ice cream.

3 Jonathan, Golden Delicious or other
    cooking apples
1/3 cup brown sugar, packed
one 2-inch cinnamon stick
1/4 tsp. nutmeg
pinch ground cloves
1 bottle (12 oz.) honey raspberry ale

Peel, core and cut apples into eighths. Combine remaining ingredients in a large heavy 3-quart saucepan and bring to a boil over high heat. Add apples and return mixture to a boil. Reduce heat to low and simmer for 12 to 15 minutes, until apples are tender. Stir occasionally while cooking. Serve hot, warm or at room temperature.

Many breweries now produce special holiday or Christmas beers. No great effort is made to maintain consistency, so beers vary slightly from year to year. Several are flavored with cinnamon, cloves, nutmeg or more exotic spices and flavorings.

TRIPLE BOCK BAKED APPLES

The flavors of triple bock are reminiscent of rich madeira, cream sherry and chocolate, which are very complementary to baked apples. Taste the beer you are going to use and if it isn't very sweet, add a tablespoon of brown sugar or maple syrup. These apples are delicious by themselves or with a dollop of sweetened whipped cream or a scoop of ice cream.

4 Rome or other baking apples
3 tbs. brown sugar, packed
3 tbs. coarsely chopped pecans
1/4 tsp. cinnamon
1-2 tsp. butter
1/2 cup Triple Bock

Heat oven to 350°. Core apples and remove peel from the top third of apple. In a small bowl, combine brown sugar, pecans and cinnamon and spoon into center of apples. Dot with butter. Place apples in a small baking dish just large enough to hold them. Pour in beer, cover dish with foil and bake for 30 to 45 minutes, until apples are tender, but not mushy. Baste occasionally with cooking liquid while baking. Serve warm or at room temperature.

DRIED FRUIT AMBER ALE COMPOTE

Choose dried apples, pears, apricots, peaches, prunes or mixed dried fruits to make this deliciously sweet dessert. If you like, top with a small amount of vanilla yogurt, whipped cream or vanilla ice cream. This recipe doubles easily and makes a great brunch dish, too.

1 bottle (12 oz.) amber ale
¼ cup sugar
2 quarter-sized pieces ginger root,
    unpeeled

one 2-inch cinnamon stick
3-4 whole black peppercorns
1 pkg. (8 oz.) dried fruit

Pour ale into a medium saucepan. Add sugar, ginger, cinnamon stick and peppercorns and bring to a boil; stir to dissolve sugar. Add dried fruit, cover, reduce heat to low and simmer for 10 to 15 minutes, until fruit is plump and tender. Remove from heat. Cool fruit in cooking liquid before refrigerating. Serve warm, cold or at room temperature. Remove ginger, cinnamon and peppercorns before serving.

VARIATION: FRESH AND DRIED FRUIT AMBER ALE COMPOTE

After cooking dried fruit, add about 1 cup fresh or frozen blueberries or raspberries, or some orange segments and cook for 1 to 2 additional minutes.

RASPBERRY LAMBIC ICE CREAM FLOATS

Belgian fruit-flavored lambics have intense fruit flavors and make delicious desserts. If you have leftover raspberry puree, spoon it over fresh strawberries.

1 basket (½ pt.) fresh raspberries
2 tbs. sugar
1 bottle (12 oz.) Belgian raspberry lambic (framboise)
1 pt. vanilla ice cream

Reserve a few pretty raspberries for garnish and puree remaining raspberries with a blender or food processor. Press fruit through a sieve to remove the seeds and stir in sugar. Combine 2 tbs. of the raspberry lambic with 2 tbs. of the ice cream in the bottom of 2 or 3 tall glasses. Stir until mixture is creamy. Add 2 tbs. raspberry puree to each glass and top with remaining ice cream. Fill glasses with raspberry lambic and garnish with reserved raspberries. Serve immediately with straws and long iced tea spoons.

PEACH MELBA WITH RASPBERRY LAMBIC

Servings: 4

This is an adaptation of a classic dessert using Belgian raspberry lambic. The raspberry puree can be made a day or two ahead and refrigerated.

1 cup fresh raspberries
1 tbs. sugar
1 pt. vanilla ice cream
4 canned cling peach halves, or poached fresh
    peach halves
1 cup Belgian raspberry lambic (framboise)
½ cup whipped cream, optional

Puree raspberries with a blender or food processor and press through a sieve to remove the seeds. Stir in sugar. Divide ice cream among 4 dessert bowls. Top ice cream with a peach half, round-side up. Divide raspberry puree among dessert dishes and pour 2 to 3 tbs. of the raspberry lambic into each bowl. Spoon a small amount of whipped cream over the top, if using, and serve immediately.

Belgium produces more types of fermented grain beverages than any other country. It makes a range of lagers and ales very similar to those produced in the United Kingdom and Germany, as well as unique double- and triple-fermented ales, lambics and fruit-flavored lambics.

ENTERTAINING WITH BEER

BEER AND FOOD PARTIES

Beer parties can be as simple or elaborate as time and resources permit, ranging from serving items picked up at the deli to slow-cooking a spicy pot of chili or beef stew. Invite your friends, open 5 or 6 different types of beer and serve some great food. Or, enlist each of your guests to bring a dish and 3 or 4 different beers for a potluck. For a simple beer-tasting party, serve cubes of bread and mild cheese, such as Monterey Jack or creamy havarti, for "palate cleansers." Pretzels and lightly buttered and salted popcorn also work well. There is no need for complicated rating systems, but do encourage your guests to talk about what they like and dislike about each beer, and to think about good food accompaniments. After the tasting, serve bowls of chili, hearty lentil and sausage soup, or a platter of grilled sausages and a green salad. Finish the evening with dessert and coffee.

You can also conduct a survey of world-class beers in order to introduce the less experienced to beers that are generally accepted to be fine examples of their type. Drink these in the order listed and serve at the suggested temperatures. Include a classic pilsner, such as Pilsner Urquell, at about 45°; a German pilsner, such as Eku Klumbacher Pils, at about 45°; a brown ale, such as Samuel Smith's Nut Brown Ale, at about 55°; a Belgian ale, such as Duvel Ale, at about 50°; an Irish stout, such as Guiness, at about 60°; a Belgian lambic (fruit ale), such as framboise (raspberry), at about 50°; and a strong dessert bock, such as Samuel Adams Triple Bock, at about 65°.

BEER PARTY MENUS

Searching for perfect beer and food matches can be a pleasurable lifetime pursuit, because it is what *you* like that counts. Since beer goes well with so many things, you can't go wrong with a beer and food party. Invite your friends to bring some interesting beers to taste or their own special party dish.

BEER AND CHEESE PARTY

Select several cheeses and pair them with beer, or ask your guests to discover their own preferred matches. Serve a variety of breads, crackers and seasonal fruit, such as apples, pears and grapes. In general, strong cheeses go better with strong, dark beers.

Brie with dry stout or Belgian lambic
cheddar with amber ale or bitter
aged cheddar with brown ale
Gorgonzola with oatmeal stout or marzen
Gruyère with brown ale
Muenster with an abbey-type ale
Roquefort with porter or stout
Stilton with porter or marzen

SIMPLE DELI PARTY

For easy entertaining, make a dish or two or a dessert and pick up the rest of the food from your supermarket or deli.

salad greens from the salad bar, or packaged salad greens
rotisserie chicken or roasted chicken pieces
German-Style Potato Salad, page 46, or *Stout Baked Beans*, page 63
bakery rolls
Chocolate-Raspberry Beer Cake, page 152
beers: amber ale or oatmeal stout with the meal; framboise lambic with dessert

GRILLED LAMB BARBECUE

Beer goes with almost any party food.

Middle Eastern Appetizer Plate with *Pita Chips*, pages 22 and 23
Lager-Marinated Mushrooms, page 24
Cherry tomato and/or radish crudités
Charcoal-Grilled Leg of Lamb, page 130
Almond and Dried Cherry Pilaf, page 69
Green Bean and Mushroom Salad, page 47
ice cream with assorted toppings
beers: brown ale, marzen

CURRY PARTY

Beer is the perfect accompaniment for spicy curries.

Tomato Pork Curry, page 124
condiments: assorted chutneys,
    chopped peanuts, toasted coconut
hot steamed rice

fresh fruit salad with oranges and
    pineapple
Raspberry Lambic Ice Cream Floats,
    page 159
beers: India pale ale, Scotch ale

CHILI PARTY

Chili is even better when made a day ahead and reheated.

vegetable tray with dip
Chili served in individual toasted *Bread
    Bowls*, page 112
Stout Gingerbread, page 155

fruit and cheese plate with pears, apples,
    aged Gouda or manchego, Brie
beers: bock, pale ale, dark Mexican lager

BACKYARD OR BEACH PARTY

This is a great 4th of July party menu. Reheat the chicken pieces on the grill.

Shrimp Boiled in Beer, page 31
grilled sausages and oysters
Spicy Braised Chicken Legs, page 94
sweet corn

Red Cabbage and Fennel Slaw, page 48
bakery rolls
watermelon wedges
beers: lager, hefe-weisen

SUPER BOWL PARTY

This menu can be made ahead. Warm the chicken wings for a few minutes just before serving.

Spicy Indian Eggplant Spread, page 20
Santa Fe Chicken Wings, page 28
Italian Sausage Calzones, page 114
Green Bean and Mushroom Salad, page 47
fresh fruit platter
Pecan-Porter Spice Cake, page 154
beers: pilsner, amber ale, North American lager

COMPANY ALE DINNER

This is delicious fare for a chilly or rainy evening.

Mustard-Marinated Shrimp, page 30
Carrot and Leek Wheat Ale Soup, page 37, or *Caesar Salad*, page 45
Roasted Pork with Brown Ale Sauce, page 126
oven-roasted potatoes and carrots
hot rolls
Peach Melba with Raspberry Lambic, page 160
beers: pale ale with shrimp; brown or golden ale with pork

INDEX

SERVE CREATIVE, EASY, NUTRITIOUS MEALS WITH nitty gritty® COOKBOOKS

Beer and Good Food
Unbeatable Chicken Recipes
Gourmet Gifts
From Freezer, 'Fridge and Pantry
Edible Pockets for Every Meal
Cooking With Chile Peppers
Oven and Rotisserie Roasting
Risottos, Paellas and Other Rice
   Specialties
Entrées From Your Bread Machine
Muffins, Nut Breads and More
Healthy Snacks for Kids
100 Dynamite Desserts
Recipes for Yogurt Cheese
Sautés
Cooking in Porcelain
Appetizers
Casseroles
The Toaster Oven Cookbook
Skewer Cooking on the Grill
Creative Mexican Cooking
Extra-Special Crockery Pot Recipes
Slow Cooking
Marinades
The Wok

No Salt, No Sugar, No Fat Cookbook
Quick and Easy Pasta Recipes
Cooking in Clay
Deep Fried Indulgences
Cooking with Parchment Paper
The Garlic Cookbook
From Your Ice Cream Maker
Cappuccino/Espresso: The Book of
   Beverages
The Best Pizza is made at home*
The Best Bagels are made at home*
Convection Oven Cookery
The Steamer Cookbook
The Pasta Machine Cookbook
The Versatile Rice Cooker
The Dehydrator Cookbook
The Bread Machine Cookbook
The Bread Machine Cookbook II
The Bread Machine Cookbook III
The Bread Machine Cookbook IV:
   Whole Grains and Natural Sugars
The Bread Machine Cookbook V:
   Favorite Recipes from 100 Kitchens

The Bread Machine Cookbook VI:
   *Hand-Shaped Breads from the
   Dough Cycle*
Worldwide Sourdoughs From Your
   Bread Machine
Recipes for the Pressure Cooker
The New Blender Book
The Sandwich Maker Cookbook
Waffles
Indoor Grilling
The Coffee Book
The Juicer Books I and II
Bread Baking (traditional)
The 9x13 Pan Cookbook
Recipes for the Loaf Pan
Low Fat American Favorites
Healthy Cooking on the Run
Favorite Seafood Recipes
New International Fondue Cookbook
Favorite Cookie Recipes
Flatbreads From Around the World
Cooking for 1 or 2
The Well Dressed Potato

For a free catalog, write or call:
Bristol Publishing Enterprises, Inc.
P.O. Box 1737, San Leandro, CA 94577
(800) 346-4889; in California, (510) 895-4461

* perfect for your bread
  machine